Service User Research in Health and Social Care

Service User Research in Health and Social Care

Hugh McLaughlin

Los Angeles • London • New Delhi • Singapore • Washington DC

SAGE Publications Ltd
1 Oliver's Yard
55 City Road
London EC1Y 1SP

SAGE Publications Inc.
2455 Teller Road
Thousand Oaks, California 91320

SAGE Publications India Pvt Ltd
B 1/I 1 Mohan Cooperative Industrial Area
Mathura Road
New Delhi 110 044

SAGE Publications Asia-Pacific Pte Ltd
33 Pekin Street #02-01
Far East Square
Singapore 048763

Library of Congress Control Number: 2008934791

British Library Cataloguing in Publication data

A catalogue record for this book is available from the British Library

ISBN 978-1-84787-071-1
ISBN 978-1-84787-072-8 (pbk)

Typeset by CEPHA Imaging Pvt. Ltd., Bangalore, India
Printed in India at Replika Press Pvt Ltd
Printed on paper from sustainable resources

Contents

Contents

Acknowledgements

In writing this book, I would like to thank all the 'service users' I have met in practice, and as a researcher, those who have educated me, challenged me and helped to shape my ideas and views over the years. I would also like to thank Susannah Trefgarne, Anne Birtchnell and Rachel Burrows from Sage for their editorial encouragement and prompt response to any query. In particular, I would like to thank Catherine, without whose love, help and support and allowing me to elude the household chores, this book would never have seen the light of day. I would also like to thank James and Eleanor for making sure I never forgot who I was!

1 The Development of Service User Involvement in Health and Social Care Research

Introduction

This book aims to provide the reader with a clear introduction to the rationale, costs and benefits, ethical considerations, ontological, epistemological, practicalities and critical issues in involving service users in research. Throughout the book you will find boxes, like the one below, which ask you to reflect on your understanding of the issues being considered. You may want to record your responses to chart your understanding of the issues as they develop throughout the book's journey.

Reflexive Questions

* When people talk of service users, what does this conjure up for you?
* What do you understand as involvement and what do you understand by the term research?

These critical issues, as you will find out, are contentious and will be visited and re-visited as we proceed through the book, unpicking assumptions, challenging received wisdoms and developing our awareness of the issues involved. By the end of the book it is intended that the reader will be able to critically assess where service user involvement would be beneficial, identify the strengths and weaknesses of such an approach, be able to justify a decision to include or exclude service users in research, identify the nature and limitations of service user knowledge claims and be able to critically evaluate other researchers' attempts at involving service users.

To begin our journey this chapter charts the development of service user involvement in policy, practice and research, exploring what we mean by health and social care, 'service users' and identifying the book's structure and organization.

Context of service user involvement

Beresford (2005), a key figure in involving service users in policy, education and research, rightly observes that we cannot begin to understand service user involvement in research without first considering user involvement more generally. He notes that there has been a growing and strengthening interest in the development of service user involvement in health and social care policy and planning since the 1980s. However, the development of service user involvement in research has been slower to develop. It is also worth noting that the development of service user involvement has been an international phenomenon, with ideas from other countries such as the USA, with its tradition of civil rights, and the developments in the Netherlands influencing the direction in the UK (Warren, 2007).

The Conservative governments of Thatcher and Major had been keen to reduce the power of professionals who were viewed as operating health and social care services for their own ends and wanted to move towards more customer centred organizations run by professional managers. Following the election of the Labour government in 1997 this trajectory was further enhanced with the introduction of the modernization thesis. Modernization (Department of Health, 1998a) is viewed as the necessary process for updating public services, including health and social care, to match the expectations of the modern day consumer. As such, it maintained the Conservatives' attack on provider dominance whilst promoting business solutions to social policy problems and sharpening accountability (Newman, 2000). Modernization emphasized the importance of developing partnerships (Balloch and Taylor, 2001) and taking user involvement seriously, as well as requiring agencies to work with, and develop partnerships with those for whom they provided services. This emphasis on service user partnerships and involvement can be seen in a range of government publications, including Department of Health, 1998a, 2000a, 2000b, 2005; NHS Executive, 1999; and in the range of national service frameworks, for example, mental health, older people, children (Department of Health, 1999, 2001b; Department of Health and Department for Education and Skills, 2004) and the *Valuing People* strategy for people with learning difficulties (Department of Health, 2001c). In a more recent initiative the government has been establishing local involvement networks (LINks) in adult services whose remit includes the encouragement and support of local people to become involved in how local health and social care services are planned and run (Department of Health, 2007a). Importantly, LINks will look at all health and social care services within a geographical area irrespective of whether they are provided by the NHS, a local authority, a private company, a social enterprise or a charity. LINks will also have the right of entry to a range of services to examine what they do. It is too early to know whether LINks will be effective or not, but they represent an attempt to bridge the normal health and social divide whilst promoting public involvement.

The UK government has been keen to promote service user and carer involvement in social policy and service development, but this has often been more a question of ideology rather than one of definitive evidence. Crawford et al. (2002) have identified that the involvement of patients has contributed to the changes in the provision of services across a range of settings, but there is little evidence as to how these changes have impacted upon the quality of care or the health of patients. Simpson and O'House (2002: 1265), in a systematic review, identified five randomized control trials and seven other comparative studies, mainly involving studies in the United States of America, whereby they concluded that:

> users can be involved as employees, trainers, or researchers without detrimental effect. Involving users with severe mental disorders in the delivery and evaluation of services is feasible.

This is hardly a ringing endorsement for the involvement of service users and carers and the situation is not very different within the social care field where a Social Care Institute for Excellence (SCIE) review stated:

> Efforts to involve people in the planning and development of services they use are taking place across the UK. However, the impact of that participation on the change and improvement of social care services is yet to be properly monitored and evaluated. (Carr, 2004: v)

The position within health and social care on the involvement of service users and carers in the social policy and service development is that it is a widely supported and welcomed development, but there remains little evidence to back this support in relation to improving health or social care outcomes.

Alongside these developments in social policy there have been similar developments in education and training in health and social care. These have included the representation of service users and carers on the management committee of the General Social Care Council (GSCC) (Hasler, 2003), involvement in the development and the approval of health care professions (Health Professions Council, 2003), nursing (Nursing and Midwifery Council, 2004), social work courses at pre-and post-qualifying levels (Department of Health, 2002; GSSC, 2005) and the involvement of service users and cares in the planning and delivery of health and social care education (Hanson and Mitchell, 2001; Citizens as Trainers, 2004; McGarry and Thom, 2004; Bassett et al., 2006;

Beresford et al., 2006). This is not to say that involving service users in education and training is not without its difficulties. Bassett et al. (2006) and Tyler (2006) rightly observe there are a number of potential barriers to involvement, including gaining access, lack of time for preparation, academic jargon, emphasis upon academic knowledge, individualized nature of higher education, discrimination and payment systems. Many of these reasons, as we will see later, are reflected in the barriers to involving service users and carers in research.

❖ Democratic approach

Alongside this development of service user involvement from the managerialist perspective in social policy and education there has also been a significant strand of development from what Beresford (2005) describes as the democratic approach. This approach is intimately linked with the personal experience of service users and carers who, having experienced services, want to have a greater say in how services are configured and delivered so that they can have a greater say in controlling their own lives (Beresford and Croft, 1996). This democratic approach implies a redistribution of power. This is something that it is not included with the more managerialist approach, which is about effectiveness, efficiency and economy with no suggestion that those with power should either seek to share or relinquish their power bases. In fact it could be argued that the opposite is true whereby service user and carer involvement is seen to establish credibility or to provide a managerial mandate.

The development of the democratic approach can be seen in the development of the disability movement and their response to Le Court, Cheshire Home (Barnes and Mercer, 1997). The disabled residents of this residential home asked expert researchers Miller and Gwynne (1972) to support them in taking greater control of their everyday lives. The researchers quickly alienated the residents, rejected their complaints and produced a report after three years recommending a re-working of traditional approaches. The residents felt betrayed and several of them later helped to establish the Union of Physically Impaired Against Segregation (UPIAS) in 1976. UPIAS became central to the development of the social model of disability, critiquing experts and professionals who claimed to speak on the behalf of disabled people who, in UPIAS's opinion, only pursued their own interests:

> We as a Union are not interested in descriptions of how awful it is to be disabled. What we are interested in is the ways of changing our conditions of life, and thus overcoming the disabilities which are imposed on top of our physical impairments by the way this society is organised to exclude us. (UPIAS, 1976)

This early concern by the disability movement was later taken up those with mental health difficulties and learning disabilities. More recently Wilson and Beresford (2000) have accused professionals of:

- appropriating user's knowledge;
- using and reinforcing inherently oppressive knowledge about service users, for example, a bio-medical model of madness and distress;
- reinforcing constructions of 'clients' as passive and low status by controlling the ideas of 'anti-oppressive practice' and knowledge of 'oppression';
- mirroring and masking traditional professional power;
- providing continued legitimation for controlling and problematic social work practice. (Wilson and Beresford, 2000: 569–70)

The democratic approach represents an alternative but significant discourse, challenging the orthodoxy of the managerialist approach whose power to describe and classify is often left unquestioned.

Health and social care

At this stage it is helpful to clarify some key terms and we will begin by examining what is meant by health and social care.

Reflexive Questions

✳ What do you think about when someone talks about health and social care? Specifically, who are the people/professions you normally refer to when you think of health and social care?

Health and social care are major employers in the UK with an identified work-force of 1.3 million employed in the NHS in 2006 (http://www.ic.nhs.uk/webfiles/publications/nhsstaff2006/NHS%20Staff%20leaflet.pdf accessed 9 March 2008) and 1.83 million in social care (http://www.socialcaring.co.uk/index.php?option=com_content&task=view&id=10&Itemid=8 accessed 9 March 2008). As such, health and social care have a substantive impact on the UK economy, not only by the nature of their tasks but also as major employers.

When you considered the first part of this question you might have included health workers as being all those people who are employed by the health service and private health care agencies; for social care those employed by local authorities, voluntary or private agencies to deliver care to promote individuals' welfare. Those involved in health care include: doctors, nurses, radiographers, midwives, health visitors, district nurses, dentists, psychologists, physiotherapists, dieticians, public health experts, occupational therapists and community psychiatric nurses. Their workplaces are normally associated with hospitals, GP surgeries or health centres. However, where do the chiropractors or complementary medicines fit in, and what do we mean by health? Downie and Telfer (1980), in a philosophical exploration of health and social work, saw health not as one but as two oppositions, that is between health and disease or illness on the one hand, and between good and poor health on the other. In their view illness or disease is seen as an episode, interrupting health which will later be restored when the illness or disease has passed. Poor health, on the other hand, suggests a long-lasting disposition to regularly being or becoming ill. A healthy person, by contrast, is someone who does not suffer from poor health and may even be described as normally healthy, even when they are ill. There are, however, clear cases where poor health is not due to disease or an illness but to some other factor, such as a defective heart or malnutrition.

Traditionally medicine has been more concerned with disease than with health. For most medical professionals disease has been conceptualized in biomedical terms as a deviation from the norm: the normal peak flow capacity of our lungs or normal blood pressure. However, having a disease does not necessarily mean that you would feel ill. High blood pressure, not caused by any particular disorder, if when found on examination would be diagnosed as a 'disease' even though the patient would not be aware that they were 'ill'. Blood pressures are measured over a continuum and will vary over time and there is no clear-cut unambiguous high blood pressure that presents a threat to health.

> In fact, there are differences even between European countries in terms of treatment for blood pressure. In Germany, for instance, low blood pressure is taken seriously as a 'disease' and widely treated, because it is seen as responsible for such problems as chronic fatigue. In Britain, few doctors would treat low blood pressure as a 'disease'. (Marsh and Keating, 2006: 392)

Similarly, patients may suffer from an illness without an identifiable 'disease'. A large number of people who visit their general practitioner suffer with symptoms such as tiredness or nausea which cannot be diagnosed as caused by an illness. This is further complicated by debates over the realities of conditions such as attention deficit hyperactivity disorder or repetitive strain injury (RSI). This is problematized further when we remember that homosexuality was declassified as a 'disease' only following a vote at the American Psychiatric Association in 1973 (Morgan et al., 1983).

We also need to remember about the significant social basis for health:

Individuals from higher socioeconomic positions are on average healthier, taller and stronger, and live longer than those lower down the scale. (Giddens, 2001: 45)

Whilst there is agreement that there is a connection between health and social inequalities, there is no agreement about what that connection is. Debate has focused on the relative importance of individual variables like lifestyle, single parenthood, diet or cultural patterns, as opposed to more structural explanations such as social class or income distribution.

We have examined concepts of health from a philosophical, biomedical and social perspective from which we can state quite clearly that health and disease are not unambiguous, but contested concepts. We will also see later that many disability groups reject the medicalized model of health for a social model of disability (Oliver, 1996). We will now look at the position of social care.

A social care worker normally refers to social workers, social service officers, rehabilitation officers, residential workers, youth offending officers and family centre workers. Social care, like health, covers the life cycle and focuses on those who are in some need of help which can be provided via family support services, residential care, foster care, daycare or any combination of the aforementioned. Social care and social work are not synonymous terms but have increasingly become conflated. Social care usually refers to all those who work within social services whether in a statutory, voluntary or private agency. Unlike health there is currently no equivalent of the private health care market; social workers do not have private patients. There are, however, private providers of services which are commissioned by local authorities and private recruitment agencies who provide social care workers. Social workers, although only a small percentage of the social care workforce (5.4% http://www.socialcaring.co.uk/index.php?option= com_content&task=view&id=10&Itemid=8 accessed 9 March 2008), are often considered to be at the forefront of social care. To be called a social worker a worker needs to have completed an approved academic programme involving both academic and practice elements and to be registered with the GSCC. Currently only social workers and students attending a registered social work training course can register, although it is intended that other social care workers, starting with domiciliary workers, will be registered in the near future. In *Options for Excellence*, a government position statement on social work in England, social work was described as:

a problem solving activity, carried out by the worker through relationships with the individual, families and community. Social work is usually needed when individuals, families or groups are facing a major and often life changing problem or challenge.

Social workers help individuals and families to achieve the outcomes they want in the ways they prefer. (Department of Health and Department of Education and Skills, 2006: 49)

This is in contrast to the international definition of social work supported by the International Federation of Social Workers (IFSW) and the International Association of Schools of Social Work (IASSW) who claim:

The social work profession promotes social change, problem solving in human relationships, and the empowerment and liberation of people to enhance well-being. Utilising theories of human behaviour and social systems, social work intervenes at points where people interact with their environments. Principles of human rights and social justice are fundamental to social work. (IAASW and IFSW, 2004) (www.ifsw/en/p38000208.html accessed 3 July 2007)

The two definitions, whilst having much in common, also have some clear differences. Both emphasize the importance of human relationships for the promotion of problem solving and change. The UK government's definition, however, stops short of promoting the 'liberation of people' or the promotion of 'social justice' although in the lines following the quote it does acknowledge the importance of human rights. This tension between the personal and social has been a constant source of friction since the introduction of social workers. The UK government's definition also promotes the desire to 'help individuals achieve the outcomes they want in the way they prefer'. This is a clear statement supporting service user involvement in social care to promote service user control. There are, however, some difficulties with this view, as it cannot be seen as an absolute – or how would be able to deal with situations where there are competing interests. For example, in child protection situations, the decision to remove a child from its parents may be justified by the needs of the child and the parents' inability to care for that child; but such a move may be totally in opposition to what the parents want. Similarly, a daughter caring for her mother may require her mother to receive respite care to allow her to continue to care for her mother, but it may well not be what the mother wants or would prefer to happen.

At this point it is tempting to suggest that health and social care are incommensurate activities. Health is a universal service, free at the point of delivery, whilst social work and social care are selective services for which individuals may be charged, based on their ability to pay. It is possible to exit the health service and go privately but such an option is not possible for social care clients. However, with the development of direct payments and the promotion of a personalization agenda, service users are increasingly able to design, manage and pay for services which meet their needs (Secretary of Sate for Health, 2006).

Whilst both services may appear incommensurate, this would be inaccurate on a number of different levels. Health and social care are inextricably bound up. The health worker and social worker can be, and must be, the ancillary worker to the other. Both health and social care are key constituents of the welfare state. Health is wanted for its own sake and the possession of it is a necessary precondition to pursue other goals. Part of the social worker role will then be to promote the health and well-being of any client or service user. For example, the Government in England and Wales made it a performance indicator for social services as part of the Quality Protects Programme (Department of Health, 1998b) to ensure that young people who were looked after by the state were receiving regular health assessments and dental treatment. As the social worker was expected to undertake holistic assessments they needed to be able to establish a working relationship with health personnel and where appropriate advocate on behalf of service users. It is also worth noting that Quality Protects required local authorities to demonstrate how they involved young people and their carers in service delivery and evaluation.

An individual may become a service user when they are unable to hold down employment due to chronic ill-health, alcoholism, drug misuse or mental ill-health. It is also true that incidents of domestic violence, child or elder abuse may come to the attention of social workers which will need the help of medical staff. For example, if an older person is admitted to hospital with physical injuries following an assault by a carer the social worker needs to undertake an assessment which includes the diagnosis, nature and severity of the injury, but also they will be seeking information about the state of the older person and carer, why the assault occurred and what can be done to reduce the risk. If the risk is too great an alternative placement for the older person may be required. Alternatively, it will be important to assess whether a single parent will recover sufficiently from their mental illness to be able, with or without support, to look after their children again, or will alternative plans for the children's long-term care be required.

Further examples of the interdependence between health and social care identified by Downie and Telfer (1980) include health's reliance on other aspects of welfare. An older person's independence may be threatened because their health is impaired due to their home being too damp, being unable to afford the electricity to heat their home, too many stairs to climb, insufficient finance and an inability to go out and shop for what they need. In cases like this it may require the health worker's expertise to identify what is needed to improve the health of the older person, but it is the social care worker's responsibility to obtain it. This type of situation can also be seen in the recent and ongoing tensions between hospitals and adult social services departments over the discharge of people from hospital who did not need to be there but remained there because nursing or homecare was not available. This later became known as 'bedblocking', which resulted in the UK government allocating £300 million to tackle this problem and the introduction of legislation to transfer funds from local authorities to hospital trusts where local authorities were seen to be 'bedblocking' (Department of Health Press Release, 2006). There are also those cases where the dependence of health on social care is even more fundamental, as in the case of psychiatric, and some physical illnesses, which appear to be bound up in family or personal problems where the need for social work is integral not only in alleviating the symptoms but also in understanding the condition.

It is intended in this initial section to highlight that, although conceptually and in common discourse we often emphasize the points of difference between health and social care services, there is in reality a large degree of interdependence. Rather than health and social care being seen as mutually competitive and antagonistic each is often dependent upon the skills of the other. Certainly this is the view of service users who are often more concerned about the provision of a service than who provides it.

Having looked at health and social care, it is now important to look at how we conceptualize those to whom health and social care services are offered, in particular to unpick what we mean when we talk about patients, clients, consumers, experts by experience and service users.

Patients, clients, consumers, experts by experience and service users

Reflexive Questions

* Before the chapter goes on to examine the importance of how people who use services are described, how would you describe the relationships that are identified by the terms: patient; client; consumer; experts by experience; service user.

* If you were receiving services from a mental health or physical disability team, which term would you prefer to be identified by? Is there another term you would like to see adopted?

Patient, client, expert by experience and service user all represent terms by which we identify one part of the health and social care relationship with those with whom they are expected to work. Patient is probably the easiest of the terms to identify in that it is likely we have all been patients and at least visited our GP, even if we have been lucky enough not to require treatment. Being a patient is associated with health care, although the early almoners, early forms of social workers found in hospitals, also called their clients patients.

It is worthwhile noting at this early stage that it is dangerous and inaccurate to 'other' the health or social care relationship. Medical personnel can also be patients, and it is highly likely that most of us will come into contact with social care services, either for ourselves, our parents, partners or children. In reading about patients, service users or experts by experience, there is often a dualism, suggesting that there are two different species, i.e. those who deliver services and those who receive them. Such a view, however, is too simplistic, and we need to remember that we all play multiple roles and that medical personnel may in one situation be the expert and in the next the patient. The two statuses are not mutually incompatible.

❖ *Patients*

The use of the term 'patient' has a long history and is in common use today. It is usually associated with the biomedical model and the application of science to medical diagnosis and the cure. According to Giddens (2001) there are three main assumptions which underpin the biomedical model of health. First, disease is viewed as a breakdown in the body's normal state. Thus, in order to restore the body to its normal state the cause of the disease must be located and treated. Second, there is a strict dualism between mind and body in which the patient presents as a 'sick body', pathology, rather than as a whole person. The individual's well-being is a secondary consideration to treating the disease and curing the sick body. In this way the patient can be investigated and manipulated ignoring external factors and promoting a detached, neutral and scientific approach. Third, within this approach only those who are trained professionals are considered as experts in the treatment of disease. The hospital represents the natural environment for the practice and pursuit of medicine where the treatments of serious illnesses often include a combination of medication, technology, or surgery.

In recent years this biomedical model has increasingly come under criticism. It has been claimed that the scientific effectiveness of medicine has been overrated as developments like effective sanitation, better housing, nutritional advances and improved hygiene have been significantly more important than developments in surgery. Illich (1976), a radical political and social theorist in critiquing modernization and the corrupting influence of institutions, claimed that modern medicine had actually done more harm than good. Traditional forms of healing and knowledge were discounted or seen as inferior to the medicalization of health and the rise of the expert.

Secondly, and significantly for our considerations, has been the critique of the mind–body split. Within the biomedical model medicine is based on scientific approaches in which the patient is a 'sick body' to be treated and cured and there is therefore little need to take account of the patient's views of their condition or treatment. The critique argues that the patient's views and experiences of their illness are crucial to a successful treatment. The patient, far from being merely a 'sick body', is a whole person whose overall well-being is an important factor in their treatment.

Attached to this there is a critique of the supremacy of medicine as the arbiter of 'scientific truth' as displayed by the increase in patients willing to pay for alternative or complementary medicines such as homeopathy and acupuncture. Lastly, there is a critique of the hospital as the primary environment for the treatment of illnesses, which has resulted in the medicalization and appropriation of conditions like pregnancy. Childbirth, far from being seen as a natural phenomenon managed by women with the help of midwives in their own homes, now occurs in hospitals overseen by medical specialists, many of whom are male.

Both the biomedical model and its critique have been described here as ideal types (Marsh and Keating, 2006) in that the two typologies have been constructed as analytical models emphasizing certain traits. Neither model exists in its totality; many medical personnel are aware that how patients feel can have an impact upon their illness, and those who use alternative medicines may still visit their doctor when they are ill. The two models do, however, throw into sharp relief differing interpretations of what it means to be a patient. Within the biomedical model the patient is passive with no active part to play except as being the host for a disease which a clinical expert then diagnoses and cures. The only activity for the patient to do is to follow the doctor's orders and do what they say in terms of rest, exercise or taking a particular medication. In the second model, the patient is more active in that the health care worker views the patient holistically whose well-being in the broadest sense can positively interact with their ability to recover from their disease. In this model the patient's views of how they are and how the treatment is experienced are important. The power, however, still remains firmly in the hands of the medical expert to define who is, and who is not, a patient. This model, although an improvement on the biomedical model in relation to service user and carer involvement, is still limited and limiting.

❖ Clients

When I entered social work in the late 1970s the most common way of referring to the social worker's relationship with those with whom they worked was via the term 'client'. As McDonald (2006) notes, this is still probably the most common way that the relationship is framed around the globe. The term client, like patient, implies a passive relationship wherein the social worker was seen as the expert who could assess what people needed and then provided for their needs. This was a very paternalistic relationship in which the client's role was to answer the social worker's questions and to do what they were requested.

At this juncture, it is worthwhile asking: Does any of this matter? It is the contention of this book that how we refer to those who use health and social care services is important. The terms we use are not merely dictionary definitions but conjure up differing identities, implying different assumptions and identifying differing power relationships.

> The words we use to describe those who use our services are, at one level, metaphors that indicate how we conceive them. At another level such labels operate discursively, constructing both the relationship and the attendant identities of people participating in the relationships, inducing very practical and material outcomes. (McDonald, 2006: 115)

Words thus act as signifiers, constructing and fixing labels such as 'patient', 'client', 'consumer' 'expert by experience' or 'service user'. Each of these signifiers implies a slightly different relationship with differing nuances and differing power dynamics; thus, how we refer to those who use the services of health and social care personnel is important.

❖ Consumers and customers

In social work and to a lesser extent in health services, the structural changes epitomized by the Children Act (1989) and the NHS and Community Care Act (1990) heralded the change from clients to consumers or customers. The introduction of these two Acts into social services resulted in the fragmentation of services and subjected social services unevenly to the disciplines of the mixed economy of care. The role of social services became redefined from both assessor and provider of care to that of 'commissioner' or 'enabler', whereby social services were expected to identify a person's needs and then purchase the services to meet those needs from the voluntary and private sector as well as from the public sector.

In adult social care services social workers became care managers and 'clients' became 'customers' or 'consumers'. This change represented a shift from the view of the client receiving services from a paternalistic state to the identity of a 'customer' or 'consumer' who was deemed to be able to exercise rational choice and exit from any particular provider if their needs were not being met to their satisfaction. This discourse of consumers and customers was never as fully thoroughgoing in children's services as it was in adult services. Children and young people could not choose which residential provider they desired nor could they decide to change a child safeguarding assessment if they did not like the outcome. In recent years there has also been some questioning as to whether the changes have been as thoroughgoing in adult services as we have been led to believe (Kirkpatrick, 2006).

The alternative identity of 'consumer' or 'customer' assumes the ideal consumer or customer is one who is rationally able to exercise their rights within a marketized and managed service. There are, however, a number of flaws in this model. For example, if we assume that if people acted rationally they would not engage in behaviours which damaged their health. However, we know that people do not always do what is good for them: you just have to think about the numbers of people you know who continue to smoke or 'binge' drink even though they know their health is being damaged. McDonald (2006) also suggests that this new discourse creates a division between those who are able to choose between a range of options, including public, voluntary or private providers 'buying' in services to meet their own needs. In contrast, there are those who are unable to pay and are thus welfare dependent that exist oppositionally to those with the resources to pay and are seen as morally defective and excluded from other desirable identities.

❖ Service users

In recent years the primacy of 'consumer' and 'customer' has been replaced by the notion of the service user. As we have already noted, this has been promoted through both managerialist and democratic approaches. This is an attempt to represent an alternative identity and to identify an alternative relationship mode. This new relationship sought to represent those who received services as service users who had a right to have a say in the services they received. The identification of service users within the modernization process represented a challenge to professionals who were seen as too powerful and too concerned with organizing services to suit themselves as opposed to those they were supposed to serve.

However, there are a number of concerns about the use of the term 'service user'. In particular this critique will highlight the limitations of viewing an individual through the prism of one aspect of their life, the neglect of those who are entitled to a service but do not take it up, the involuntary nature of certain services, the development of multi-disciplinary teams and the development of Direct Payments and the personalization agenda.

Shaping Our Lives, a national service user network, has questioned the use of the term 'service user':

> The term 'service user' can be used to restrict your identity as if all you are is a passive recipient of health and welfare services. That is to say, a service-user can be seen as someone who has things 'done to them' or who quietly accepts and receives a service. This makes it seem that the most important thing about you is that you use or have used services. It ignores all the other things you do and which make up you as a person. (Shaping Our Lives Network, 2003 quoted in Warren, 2007: 8)

Service users are viewed through the prism of their service user status. This means a service user is identified by what it was that led them to become a service user and this can include a disability, a mental health issue or a child who is looked after. The term 'service' user ascribes meaning and status by focusing on the reason for the service user status and in the process neglecting all other aspects of their life. The same individual may be a mother, manager, volunteer, school governor or magistrate, but it is their status as a service recipient that marks them out when we talk of service users. Such a perspective identifies only one aspect of their lives, an aspect that puts them into an inferior position with service providers. Being a mother, manager, volunteer, school governor or magistrate is a higher status than being a service user.

The use of the term 'service user' can also be criticized for neglecting those who, for whatever reason, are either unable to access the services they are entitled to or do not use the services they require for fear of stigma. The Sainsbury centre for Mental Health (SCMH, 2002: 3) identified a 'circle of fear' that resulted in black and minority ethnic groups avoiding mental health services for fear of racism, resulting in further deterioration of their conditions. If our research accesses only those who already use services we may be missing important information and data as to how thresholds are implemented or how services are viewed. Focusing solely on service users raises the possibility that services are not meeting the needs of those for whom the services were developed.

According to Cowden and Singh (2007) the term 'service user' begins to fall apart when we seek to use it in practice. Its usefulness becomes limited and boundaried when we consider it in relation to the more invasive and controlling aspects of service delivery. Social workers are expected to both work in partnership with service users, but also to act to protect and safeguard the vulnerable. Social workers are expected to act on their assessments informed by agency procedures and legal statutes when they consider a child to be at risk. It is unlikely that those whose lives are the subject of such interventions, especially the parents or carers, see themselves as service users. The same situation is also true in cases of adult abuse or mental health admissions.

There is also an issue with multi-disciplinary teams as to how do you relate to those who use their services. If a mental health team is made up of psychologists, community psychiatric nurses, psychiatrists, occupational therapists, residential workers and social workers, how do we refer to their service recipients? A residents, service users or patients? Different professional groups have a stake in maintaining their own professional boundaries and knowledge claims, but if teams are to become integrated one agreed definition will be required.

The last part of the critique of the term 'service user' lies with the commitment of the government towards personalized care (Department of Health, 2007c) and in particular Direct Payments (Department of Health, 1996) which allows service recipients to purchase their own care rather than relying on directly provided services. The introduction of Direct Payments is the logical extension of the modernization agenda and dissatisfaction with health and social services' inability to deliver personalized services. This trend also identifies a fracture in the way we talk of service recipients as those who use direct payments are also potentially employers of personal carers or commissioners of health and social services. Those receiving direct payments are expected either individually, or with help, to manage the work and payment of personal carers and it is thus conceptually inaccurate to consider them as purely service users. This trend towards giving people greater say in how personal services are constructed and managed has profound implications for the discourse of service users.

❖ Experts by experience

Having raised a number of issues about the use of service user it is important to consider one of the alternatives currently being promoted. 'Experts by experience' is increasingly being used by a number of service recipient groups. Expert by experience is the term favoured by, amongst others, CSCI (Commission for Social Care Inspection) and NIMHE (National Institute for Mental Health in England) and the Foundation for Learning Disabilities. CSCI define an expert by experience as:

someone with experience of using social care services and includes:

- people who use services now or have done in the past;
- people who need services but haven't been offered them;
- people who need services but haven't been offered any that are appropriate;
- people living with or caring for a person who uses services.

We involve people who use services in our work and call them **Experts by experience.** (bold in original) http://www.csci.org.uk/get_involved/take_part_in_

an_inspection/become_one_of_our_experts_by_e/who_is_an_expert_by_experience.
aspx accessed 18 July 2007.

Branfield et al. (2006: 30) describe the rationale for experts by experience by identifying that:

> … service users can be the best people to tell professionals what they want and need from any particular service, because it is intended for them and their knowledge of it is based on direct experience.

On one level the use of the term 'experts by experience' reflects a situation wherein service users are asked to contribute to service and policy developments with others and are recognized for the expertise they bring to the situation. In order to reduce the power differential and to positively highlight the contribution that service users bring to these discussions it is helpful to highlight their unique and individual experience as the expertise that singles them out from the other members. Experts by experience, however, should not be confused with 'expert patients' who are identified by the Department of Health as patients who:

- feel confident and in control of their lives;
- aim to manage their condition and its treatment in partnership with health care professionals;
- communicate effectively with professionals and are willing to share responsibility and treatment;
- are realistic about the impact of their disease on themselves and their family;
- use their skills and knowledge to lead full lives.

(www.dh.gov.uk/en/Aboutus/MinisterandDepartmentLeaders/ChiefMedicalOffier/ ProgressOnPolicy/ProgressBrowsableDocument/DH_5380856) accessed 18 July 2007.

As can be seen, both definitions are driven by professionals who wish to include the recipients of their services. In the first there are no caveats about a person's experience; it is the uniqueness of each individual's experience that is valued – both positive and negative. In the second definition on expert patients there is a very different tenor to the relationship wherein the expert patient is expected to 'work in partnership with healthcare professionals', 'communicate effectively', 'share responsibility' and 'are realistic'. All these caveats beg the question as to who decides whether someone is working in partnership, communicating effectively, sharing responsibility and being realistic, never mind using their skills 'to lead full lives'. From the Department of Health's definition this would appear to be within the gift of health care professionals. At best expert patients symbolize a reluctant acceptance by health care professionals to accept lay-led self-management of chronic conditions and at the worst a means of saving resources for the National Health Service.

The CSCI definition, agreed by the GSCC and SCIE, of experts by experience, goes some way to answering some of the questions raised in our critique of use of the term service user. This definition not only includes those who are, or have been, service users but also those who needed services but were not offered them, those who were offered inappropriate services, or those who are living with or caring for someone who uses services. However, this wider definition is not without its own frailties. There is an inherent assumption within this definition that those who required services and were not provided with them and those who received an inappropriate service are accurate. It is not so much that the 'customer is king' but that the 'expert by experience is always right'. This is not to deny that social workers or health professionals can make mistakes in their assessments, but this is a long way from assuming that they are always wrong. To suggest 'experts by experience' are always right is to replace the tyranny of the professional by the tyranny of the expert by experience (McLaughlin, 2008). It is interesting to question whether we as members of society are willing to accept those with an acute mental illness to decide which services they will accept or not and for those young people wishing to be accommodated to decide which residential or foster home?

Within the notion of the term 'experts by experience' there is an inherent tension when we begin to tease out the limits of experience. To put this in a different way, how are we to recognize experts by experience? Who decides and what criteria do we measure them against? Are we merely to accept someone's definition of themselves as an expert by experience? In terms of experience we will all be aware of colleagues and ex-colleagues who had many years' experience but who did not appear to learn from their previous experiences. They may have had 15 years' experience but it amounted to the same year 15 times. The open-endedness of this definition is helpful in being inclusive but is at the same time problematic as it provides no criteria to identify or exclude 'experts'. This is problematic as it potentially undermines the notion providing no quality assurance or thresholds in which it is possible to assert that someone is an expert as opposed to the more neutral term service user.

The notion that all experts by experience are deemed to be equal raises further problems; say two experts by experience with very similar identified needs receive the same service but experience it very differently. One is highly pleased with the service and would like to see it expanded to others in similar circumstances as themselves whilst the other may view it very critically and like to see the service radically changed. Which of these would we view as being right? Or, could it be that both are right? To make matters more complex, what about someone who did not receive the service but wanted it; can we assume the service would have accurately met their needs? Such situations dilute the power of experts by experience, highlighting the difficulty in discriminating between services and potentially putting power back in the hands of professionals to decide whose view to accept.

Experts by experience are also open to the criticism that their expertise, like a service user, is viewed through the lens of their service use and neglects the other aspects of their lives in which they may well play more socially acceptable roles. Using the term expert in this realm attempts to address this issue to some degree, but as we have seen above it is a rather hollow claim when all experiences are treated equally and the title of expert appears to be more ideological than substantive. It is also possible that under this definition all health and social care staff could also claim to be experts by experience, further undermining the usefulness of this concept.

What does all this mean?

At the start of this section you were asked to consider how you understood the terms patient, client, consumer, service user and expert by experience. From what you have now read you will see that all these concepts and labels, whilst appearing straightforward, are complex and problematic, signifying certain aspects of relationships at the expense of others. You might also wish to reflect on whether the professions have a vested interest in describing the relationship in particular ways to promote their own professional expertise. The language we use is more than the words we identify. Health and social care professionals not only use knowledge and language to help, but also as a means to define the object of their work in the form of a general concept of a patient, client, consumer, service user or expert by experience:

> Discourse is about more than language. Discourse is about the interplay between language and social relationships, in which some groups are able to achieve dominance for their interests in the way in which the world is defined and acted upon. (Hugman, 1991: 37)

We discussed at the beginning of this chapter that the international definition of social work highlights notions of social change and social justice whilst promoting empowerment. If we also accept that health is more than the absence of illness it is then essential that social work, and health, should be in a continuous dialogue concerning the language they use and the discourses they develop and are situated within. This means social work and health must be continuously challenging themselves, deconstructing and unearthing the assumptions behind their assumptive worlds. As we have seen, there is no one term that accurately captures the nature of the social work or health relationship; all the terms we identified were seen to be both contentious and problematic. This is not to suggest that there is another term out there waiting to be identified or discovered. It may be possible that terms like 'active consumers', 'responsible consumer citizens' may be adopted in the future, but this book is not about championing one or other term but about being clear how the terms we use help to shape how we conceive and understand certain relationships and thus provide an indicator as to how we should behave in such relationships. One alternative would be invent a new word altogether. Maybe you would like to try and invent your own word which you feel accurately reflects the nature of the social work or health care relationship. This, I would suggest, would still suffer from the same difficulties and contain its own assumptive worlds, which would be more or less accurate depending on the situation it was describing.

At this point the reader would be forgiven for thinking there is no right answer. In many ways there is not, but to move the situation forward we should consider first asking those who use services how they want to be identified and to respect their definition. Secondly, we as students, health workers, social workers and academics need to be more specific in the terminology we advocate and be aware of both its strengths and limitations. It may even be appropriate to use certain terms in certain situations and different terms in different situations (McLaughlin, 2008). It may also be pertinent to use different terms in the same article or lecture to highlight to audiences that all terms are contextually specific, socially constructed and not fixed. Lastly, it is important to remember that whether you use the term service user or not you are talking about a person first and foremost.

It is the intention to use the term service user throughout this book for ease of reading and also as this is the most commonly used term at present, although it is unlikely to be five years from now.

Summary

In this, the first chapter of the book, we have laid the groundwork for much of what is to come in later chapters. In particular we have highlighted the context of service user involvement in policy, practice and education of health and social workers. We have identified how both democratic and managerial approaches have provided drivers for the promotion of service user involvement against a political background that has seen professionals as delivering services more geared to their professional requirements than the needs of those they were seeking to help. We have questioned the common understanding of health and social care, highlighting both the independent and interdependent nature of each concept. It could also be argued that in relation to children's services we should also have highlighted the position of education in relation to children and young people; however, this will be developed in Chapter 7.

Having deconstructed health and social care we then took a closer look at key terms like patient, client, consumer, service user and expert by experience and found all these terms to be both contentious and ambiguous. We highlighted how the use of these terms helps to construct certain notions about relationships and that in this book we will use the term service user, accepting that it is not fixed and may not be the term to be used in the future.

Recommended reading

Beresford, P. and Croft, S. (1993) *Citizen Involvement: A Practical Guide for Change*, London: Macmillan. A key text for understanding the issues in relation to service user involvement.

Lowes, L. and Hulatt, I. (eds) (2005) *Involving Service Users in Health and Social Care Research*, London: Routledge. An edited collection of easy to read examples of service user involvement in research in health and social care.

Warren, J. (2007) *Service User and Carer Participation in Social Work*, Exeter: Learning matters. This book provides an easy introduction to this topic with very helpful legislative and policy framework overview.

2 | *Why Service Users Bother or Why Bother Involving Service Users in Research?*

Introduction

In this chapter we will examine why it is seen as worthwhile to involve service users in research. But first we ask the question: What do service users hope to gain by becoming involved in research? Also, we ask whether these hopes are deliverable? We then go on to explore the differing levels of service user involvement and the mandate and philosophical underpinnings for service user involvement. This will be followed by an examination of the benefits and identified costs of involving service users in research, including the costs and benefits to the service user, the lead researcher and the research.

Why do service users bother?

Reflexive Questions

❋ Before reading any further, why do you think service users become involved in research? What do you think they hope to gain from the process?

In trying to put your list together you may have thought about such issues as:

- Frustration with research.
- Desire for change in services.
- It's my right.
- Fancy being a researcher.
- Status.
- Personal needs.
- Having a voice.
- Personal development.
- To earn some money.

Torvey (2006: 6), in a literature review examining the reasons why service users get involved in research, concluded:

> The studies we looked at suggest that those that are motivated to get involved do so for a combination of reasons related to their personal situation, their experiences of health and/or social care services (often negative) as well as possibly having a more general commitment to getting involved and bringing about change.

All of us have had the experience whereby we have become frustrated with being at the receiving end of a service, such as in a restaurant, shop or even research where we have thought we could have done a better job. This is particularly likely to be the case where our experience has been negative and frustrating. In such circumstances we may wish to be the waiter, shop assistant or researcher to be able to put things right or to tell the story as it 'really is' and to bring about the changes we want to see that will make a difference. A potential service user researcher may view their involvement as an opportunity to have their voice heard where in the normal flow of everyday life their voice and views would be drowned out by those of the experts or professionals. It is important to note that people often wish to get involved in research both as service user and as academic researcher because they believe a situation or a service could, and should, be improved. This issue of a commitment to change will be dealt with further when we address the philosophical underpinnings of research in Chapter 4.

The next suggestion was that some service users may view it as their right to be involved in research that is about them. It is they who are the 'experts' on their medical condition or service and that any research that does not involve them is in danger of being at best partial and at worst misleading. This is a central tenet for the involvement of service users in research and will be re-visited and explored in greater detail throughout the book.

Alternatively, from a different perspective, we may have thought that being a researcher seemed like fun and we could do a job like that. However, it is clear that personal reasons can and do play a part in why people volunteer to become involved as service user researchers. Other personal reasons may include the idea that being a researcher is a preferred role and status in comparison to other available roles and statuses. Being a researcher provides a distraction from other life events or that being a researcher presents an opportunity to get involved in something worthwhile. There is also the possibility that some service users will view the opportunity of becoming involved in research as a potential for their own self-development and to learn new skills. Lastly, service users who volunteer to become involved as researchers may view their involvement as an opportunity to gain some financial reward and supplement their income.

Obviously, service user researchers may identify one, or more than one of the reasons identified above. It is worthwhile reflecting that it is not surprising that the reasons given for service users becoming involved in research are not very different from many of those that are likely to influence health and social care researchers.

Having identified why service users will become involved in research it is important to ask whether these aspirations are likely to be met or not. It is obviously possible, but by no means guaranteed, that we can do a better job at research than anyone else. There are a number of issues which we will discuss later as to how we can seek to ensure that research with service users has the best chances of success. However, the point is there is no guarantee that in believing you can do something better than anyone else that you will in fact be able to do so. This may be a very legitimate motivation and may help someone put in the extra effort required, but it provides no certainty of a better product. Similarly, all researchers want their research to make a difference, but again there is no guarantee that this will be the case.

Service user researchers may view being involved in research as an opportunity to have their voices heard, but this is likely to be constrained by the research process, which needs to be able to establish academic credibility and rigour for its results to be acceptable to academic, practice and policy communities. Also, once the research report is published and is in the public domain there is no guarantee of how it will be received or used. Whilst all researchers may wish their research to make an impact and to change policies or services for the better there is no assurance that this will necessarily be the case. Once the report is written and the dissemination process undertaken how individuals, agencies and organizations interpret and use the research is in their gift, not the gift of the research team.

From my experience it is quite clear that research can be fun, but it is also likely to be hard work. Whilst parts of the research process are likely to be experienced as exciting and stimulating, others are likely to be boring and hard work. As with most worthwhile tasks, it is not possible to have one without the other. Service user researchers should be able to be recompensed for their efforts in undertaking research, but there are limits to this and potential benefit issues to consider. This topic will be discussed further in Chapter 6.

It is clear from this section that those service users who volunteer to become service user researchers do so for a range of motives and there is a need to temper expectations, to ensure there is a balanced view of what can and cannot be achieved. Involvement as service user researchers is not a therapeutic intervention, a pleasure-seeking experience, alternative income strand or a mandate to change policies or services, although it may include elements of some or all of these. It is, however, very important not to oversell what can be achieved for service user researchers.

Levels of service user involvement in research

Before discussing levels of service user involvement in research it is important to examine some of the assumptions behind involving service users in the research process. Building on the work of Christensen and Prout (2002) in relation to young people, it is possible to identify a typology of service users as objects, as subjects, as social actors and as active participants. The first view represents service users as objects to be measured, collated and researched. The second viewpoint places service users in the foreground of the research able to tell their own story; however, this story is still tempered by researcher views on the validity, usefulness and competence of the service user. The third perspective sees service users as able to act, to change and be changed by their actions. In this perspective service users are seen as autonomous individuals and not merely as parts of another system or health or social care system. The last representation takes the third perspective to its logical conclusion in relation to research and sees service users as having an active part in the research process as creators and co-creators of knowledge and understanding. Within this book we attempt to examine the conditions, possibilities, strengths and weaknesses of this fourth position.

Up until now we have been discussing the involvement of service users in research as if we all agreed what that this was and as if we understood the same meaning when the term is used. This is an untenable position and we now need to become more specific about what we mean by involvement. Arnstein (1971) has probably developed the best-known model of citizen participation which suggests a ladder of eight rungs: manipulation, therapy, informing, consultation, placation, partnership, delegated power and citizen control. The first two rungs of the ladder, manipulation and therapy, are described as non-participation, whilst the next three rungs are described as tokenism with only partnership, delegated power and citizen control viewed as meaningful participation. Arnstein's linear model can be criticized for its hierarchical approach, which suggests that each rung up the ladder is better than the rung before. This is not necessarily the case and neglects the possibility that in certain circumstances different rungs may be more appropriate, depending on the nature of the activity. As Tritter and McCallum (2006) note, Arnstein's ladder fails to capture the dynamic nature of user involvement, is interested only in outcomes at the expense of processes and conflates means with ends. It is unlikely that you will have the same level of service user involvement in the research application stage as you might have in the data collection or writing-up stages. If this is the case, how would you describe the level of research involvement? There is a danger in such a model that you will either go for the highest or lowest rungs of involvement, neither of which accurately describes the degree of involvement. There is also the difficult question to answer that where you have more than one service user involved you may have differing levels of involvement. Within the model there is an assumption that you can only achieve one level, whilst in research you may in reality have a research involvement profile(s) depending on the stage of the process and the skills and abilities of the service user researcher(s).

A simpler model by Hanley et al. (2004) identified three points on a continuum: consultation, collaboration and service user controlled. Before exploring Hanley et al.'s (2004) continuum further the reader may have noted that in Hanley et al.'s model there is no room for either illusory or non-participative practices. This is a serious oversight in the model. To address this omission it is suggested that we need to add another point at the end of the continuum to capture those situations which we will call tokenistic. This term implies there is an attempt to involve service users, but this attempt, either through intent or lack of awareness, results in an illusion of involvement. For example, consider the position of a service user who volunteers to become involved in a research project only to find that the research team meetings are held at an inaccessible venue and at a time, due to child care responsibilities, they are unable to attend. In this case the researchers may well have set out to include service user researchers but that, due to a lack of thought in their planning, their actions have actually resulted in non-involvement. In such circumstances it is easy to see how service users can become cynical about a researcher's attempts to involve them. It is possible for such a situation to have been manipulated by a researcher, but such a devious approach represents unethical research and should be considered as such. It is also possible, with the increasing demand by research commissioners, to require service user involvement in bids, to include a service user's involvement as purely tokenistic. A service user researcher may be recruited to the research in order for the lead researcher to be able to tick the research commissioner's requirements but have no influence or impact on the research process at all. This would be the case when a service user is a member of a research reference group but no attempt is made to include them and the language and written material used in the reference group only serve to exclude rather than to include. It is therefore imperative that we extend Hanley et al.'s (2004) continuum. For the purposes of this book we will describe this as non-involvement to highlight the fact that although attempts have been made, through omission or commission, misguided or unintended intentions have resulted in service user non-involvement.

❖ Consultation

We are all familiar with consultation, whether this is about proposed government legislative changes, a reorganization of our work practices, a change in service, the concept for a new car or a new brand image for a well-known drink. We all experience consultation on a regular basis and will have differing views on differing occasions as to whether our opinions are either heard or acted on. Hanley et al. (2004: 8) describe consultation as:

> When you consult people who use services about research, you ask for their views to inform your decision-making. For example, you might hold one-off meetings with people who use services to ask them for their views on a research proposal. You will not necessarily adopt those people's views, but you may be influenced by them.

Hanley et al. accurately capture the inherent ambiguity of a concept like consultation. This 'useful ambiguity' (McLaughlin et al., 2004) is one of consultation's greatest strengths and allows consultation to mean different things to different people. In consultation it is 'acceptable' for a manager to consult on a particular service reorganization and to gather opinions and views from all the staff and stakeholders but for the manager not to act on any critical views and still be able to say that they have consulted. Consultation does not guarantee that any ideas, changes or issues raised by those who are being consulted will have any impact or influence whatsoever on the outcome. This is not to imply that consultations may not radically change a project, but the 'useful ambiguity' of the term does not imply that they have any influence at all for them to be legitimately described as consultation. Hanley et al. (2004) describe consultation as a safe place to begin service user involvement as it is a simple process without any promises. The power in consultation firmly resides with those undertaking the consultation to decide who should be consulted and what they should be consulted about. It is thus unsurprising that Beresford and Croft (1993) claim that certain powerless groups are over-consulted with little evidence of their opinions creating any change. Butt and O'Neill (2004) found that black and minority older people complained that they had been over-researched, with researchers often asking the same questions and/or producing the same results that had been produced 15 years ago. Understandably they did not want more research; they wanted action and to be involved at local and national levels in decisions which affected their own lives.

Consultation may be the first point of involvement on Hanley et al.'s (2004) continuum but it is also a point that is equally open to those who do not wish to share their power or to engage in meaningful involvement. It is for this reason you may be rather cynical about consultation as a means of involvement. Hanley's next point of the continuum is collaboration, which we now move onto.

❖ Collaboration

Collaboration, like consultation, is an unspecific concept occupying the ground between consultation, and service user controlled research. Collaboration, unlike consultation, implies that service users will be listened to and that you will be able to identify where their suggestions have impacted upon a research study. As such, collaboration offers a wide range of ongoing opportunities for meaningful service user researcher involvement. Service users may be involved in the writing of a research bid, membership of a steering or reference group, involved in identifying the research methods and questions to be asked, undertaking the data collection and analysis, writing-up of the research and disseminating the research findings. In other words, a collaborative approach promotes service user researchers' involvement in one, some or all aspects of the research process.

Collaboration requires the lead researcher to be more participative than is required for consultation as they are sharing their power to control the research as a means to ensure a more collaborative research process and a better quality product. Such a view moves away from a traditional 'zero sum' view of power where power is seen as a finite quantity, and for someone to give away power is to become less powerful. In participative research a zero sum view is eschewed as it is assumed that in working together the whole can be greater than the sum of the parts. Such situations are not necessarily 'win lose' but can be 'win win'.

Collaborative service user involvement in research is not without its difficulties. To undertake collaborative research is likely to be time consuming and to require extra resources, thus making the research more costly. Also, as already noted, collaborative research requires the research professionals to hand over some power and for some lead researchers this may be perceived as a disadvantage. For others, they may need to develop new skills in facilitation and negotiation. Whilst having done all this there is no guarantee that the extra time and resources will automatically secure a better result. Collaborative research provides an opportunity for the involvement of service users in research, but it is not an opportunity to be taken lightly or without due consideration to the nature of the research question, the skill set of the researchers or the resources available.

❖ *Service user controlled*

This is the opposite end point of the service user involvement in research continuum from that of tokenism. Whilst tokenism provides the service user researcher with no power, the locus of power at this point of the continuum remains very clearly within the ambit of the service user researchers. Service user controlled research presents a challenge to traditional ways of research production and ownership. Barnes and Mercer (1997) note that the traditional power of the researcher is enshrined in how researchers control the design, implementation, analysis and dissemination of research findings, often resulting in service users being treated as objects to be measured, categorized and quantified.

Reflexive Questions

* What is your initial response to the following scenario? How do you think the senior managers might feel about this?

* A group of mental health service users are granted funding to study directors of adult social services, chief executives of mental health trusts, Mind and similar large mental health charities. The service user researchers are collecting data on where such people lived, their lifestyles, how they achieved at school, the nature and length of their key relationships, their alcohol and drug use. On top of this they are also seeking to find out when they last conversed with someone with a mental health illness or last spoke to the partner of someone who had just been involuntarily admitted to a hospital. From this data the service user researchers want to be able to say something about the respondent's values and be in a position to comment on their suitability to run mental health services. (Based on Holman, 2001)

As the adaptation from Holman reminds us, researchers have power. Research is not a neutral activity; it can both empower and disempower. It is not an activity to be entered into lightly. Research and its focus can often represent a reflection of the inequalities of society whereby we find it easy to accept that the most vulnerable should be subject to research scrutiny whilst the most powerful remain aloof from such interventions in their lives.

So, what is entailed in user-led research? Essentially it is about service users determining the research focus, the research process, the interpretation of the findings, and the conclusions to be drawn for practice and policy. (Evans and Jones, 2004: 8)

Evans and Jones (2004: 8) go on to illustrate what they mean by user-controlled research by identifying 11 'who' questions:

- Who identifies and defines the issue or topic to be studied?
- Who identifies and defines the hypothesis to be tested and/or the questions to be asked?
- Who determines the methodologies to be used?
- Who undertakes the research?
- Who applies the methodologies/asks the questions?
- Who decides what, and how, to record the responses?
- Who collates and interprets the data?
- Who decides what conclusions should be drawn?
- Who decides how to present the conclusions?
- Who draws the lessons for policy and practice?
- Who follows through to see action results?

It is possible to suggest there should be a twelfth question: Who should write the research bid? For Evans and Jones' research, if it is to be service-user led research, the answer to most, if not all the questions, should be, 'service users'. There is, however, a difficulty of precision here, as what are we to make of the situation where we answer nine, eight, seven or six questions with 'service user researcher'. Or, to put it another way, how many 'who' questions do you need to answer with 'service user researcher' before research can be considered to be service user-led research? This also makes an assumption, which may well be untrue, that all aspects of the research process should be considered as of equal weight. The point to be noted is that service user-controlled research is not a simplistic notion and remains a dispute concept. Broadly, service user-controlled research implies that service users are responsible for the conduct of the research and any subsequent decision making, but this does not mean that service users have to undertake every aspect of the research process. Also, as Turner and Beresford (2005a) identified in their study, service users do not speak with a unitary voice on service user-controlled research. They found that service users disagreed about whether it should be service users who undertook the research or whether non-service user researchers could be employed as long as service users remained in control. Turner and Beresford (2005a: vi) also identify what their review identified as the aims of user-controlled research:

- The empowerment of service users and the improvement of their lives (both through the process and purpose of research).
- Being part of a broader process of making social and political change.

- Changed more equal relations of research production (where the people who carry out the research and are the subject of the research relate to each other on much more equal terms).
- Being based on social models of understanding and interpretation (like the social model of disability).

For Turner and Beresford service user-controlled research is not merely a different epistemology but is a political statement.

In comparison to the consultative and collaborative approaches service user-controlled research locates the power to make decisions firmly within the control of service users. Thus, if non-service user researchers are employed to undertake aspects of the research they are doing so in response to the directions and remit supplied by service users. There is, though, a thin line to be drawn between employing consultants who are expected to make 'suggestions' as to how certain activities can be carried out effectively and to when such 'suggestions' become less like 'suggestions' and more like decisions. This is a perennial difficulty for anyone who employs a 'consultant' for their expertise to decide when they should agree with what is being suggested and when to go with their original design. This is not to suggest any devious intent on the consultant or non-service user researcher but to raise the question how far anyone can remain in control when they do not fully understand what is happening and why.

This raises another issue for further debate and consideration. Does service user-controlled research mean that it is only those service users who are receiving that, or a similar service, that can truly be called a service user researcher? Or conversely, can someone who is receiving a service for a physical impairment be a service user researcher in a mental health project when they have never been a recipient of mental health services? This is a tricky question, as at one level it could be argued that what unites service users is that they are recipients of a service. However, it is one of the key justifications for involving service users in research that it is their understandings of the services being investigated that justifies their involvement in the process. Otherwise, it could be argued that service users who are not recipients of those services do not add anything more to the process than would non-service user researchers.

User-controlled research is not without its difficulties; it demands that non-service user researchers hand over power, and for some non-service user researchers this will at best be uncomfortable if not impossible. Some research commissioners and sponsors will not agree to such an arrangement, wanting a known non-service user researcher to be responsible for the research. User-controlled research often costs more if it is to support service users properly (Turner and Beresford, 2005a). Any results derived from the research may be viewed as 'subjective', as those who have the most to gain from the research have undertaken it. This problem of 'bias' is not something that is restricted solely to service user researchers and is also an issue for academic and other researchers.

As can be seen by this short exploration, service user-controlled research is contested and disputed and is still very much in its infancy with many questions yet to be answered. For our purposes, it represents one end of the service user involvement continuums whose individual points are not set in stone but represent a range of contested sitings, often overlapping from one point into the next. We have identified a model of four points: tokenism, consultation, collaboration and service user-controlled research. All of these, except tokenism, may represent service user involvement in research. This book is located primarily within the collaborative area of the continuum although will on occasions include both consultative and service user-controlled research. In deciding which level is appropriate for which research project in which circumstance requires the consideration of a number of issues. These issues include: the skill levels of the service user researcher and non-service user researcher, the nature of the research topic, the resources available and the research methods being operationalized. It also needs to be noted that differing levels of involvement may be appropriate within the same research, with possibly a greater involvement being experienced in the development of the research tools and undertaking interviews than might be the case in the analysis of the research if advanced quantitative or qualitative approaches are used.

Having discussed why service user researchers bother with research and seek to identify differing levels of service user researcher involvement, we now move on to ask what benefits are claimed for involving service users in research.

Benefits of involving service user researchers

Reflexive Questions

* If you were considering involving service users in research, what benefits would you be hoping to achieve for: (a) the research; (b) service user researchers; and (c) lead researcher or non-service user researcher?

* You may want to take a side of A4 and split it into three columns, one of for each of the three categories, which might make it easier to undertake the task.

There are many reasons identified in the literature why lead researchers should involve service user researchers and this section will identify these in relation to: (a) the research; (b) the service user researchers; and (c) the lead researcher. For ease of reading we will now refer to the lead researcher as opposed to non-service user researcher. This is meant to refer to a professional researcher for whom research is an expectation of their paid employment and who have undertaken an accredited research methods course. From this definition it is clear that some service user researchers will also come into this criterion and there are those who are able to wear both hats. This helps to remind us that we need to be continually sensitive and aware of the labels we use to describe others and the implications of those labels.

❖ Benefits to research and service development

There are a number of claimed benefits that are worthy of further exploration including:

- Focusing the research. It is often claimed that involving service users as co-researchers can help to focus research to ensure that it not only remains relevant for those who deliver the service but also for those on the receiving end (Young et al., 2007). In particular service user researchers may help by being able to prioritize topic areas. This is recognition that service users and carers are experts by experience (see Chapter 1). No one else can claim to have had the exact same experience as they have had of health and social care services and it is they who know where it has worked well and where it needs to improve. This also serves to ensure that the research will address service users' concerns and not merely be an academic exercise.
- Service user researchers can ensure that any research tools developed for the research, including questionnaires, interview schedules, consent or information leaflets, are worded in such a way as to be accessible to the target population. Similarly they may also advise on wording, including common expressions within the target group or the ordering of questions to best address the research question.
- Service users from hard-to-reach groups, like those who misuse drugs or who are living with stigmatizing conditions, are more likely to know where others in similar circumstances or conditions congregate, thus providing greater access to the target population. This can be further enhanced by service user researchers undertaking research interviews. Members of such groups may be sceptical or resistant towards traditional researchers and be more willing to participate if it is someone whom they feel is more likely to understand their position and views.
- The range and quality of the data can be enhanced.

- Having undertaken the data collection research, service user researchers can participate in the analysis of the results and help to ensure that crucial meanings are not misunderstood. They can also help to make connection between themes and ideas that would not be immediately relevant to a lead researcher.
- Service user researchers can help ensure that any recommendations include the unique perspective of service users which can help to develop services that are more likely to be used by other service recipients.
- Service user researchers can help with the dissemination of results. Service users speaking from their experiences of both being a service user and a researcher can have a much more profound effect than a professional researcher. The ability to be able to incorporate personal experience can be a major benefit.

❖ *Benefits to the service user researchers*

As identified in Chapter 1, we need to consider why anyone should wish to become involved in a research project, and in particular why service users bother and what is in it for them. This is not to claim that just by involving service users as co-researchers we will automatically ensure a better research product. It is, however, to suggest that there may be inherent benefits for service users being involved in research as co-researchers. In trying to identify what these benefits are you may have identified:

- The inclusion of service user researchers can enable service users to actively participate in addressing the issues that affect their, and those with similar conditions, impairments or service needs. As such, they can contribute to the improvement of the services they experience.
- Service user researchers, through training in research skills and involvement in the research project, can develop new skills, enhance self-esteem and improve their job prospects in becoming active participants in a research project (Lockey et al., 2004).
- The very act of being involved in a successful research project can improve confidence and an acknowledgement that service user experiences matter and are a legitimate expertise to bring to the research process.
- Involvement in research can empower service users.
- Remuneration is an issue we will return to in Chapter 5; however it is clear that service user researchers should be rewarded for their effort, skills and involvement.
- When the inclusion of service users' research is successful and mutual respect develops, a change of attitude is promoted that values the capabilities of service users and the roles they can play.

❖ *Benefits to academic researchers*

It should also be remembered that not only are there benefits for service user researchers, but there are also benefits for academic researchers. This form of research potentially benefits not only the research process and service user researchers, but also lead researchers.

- Increased awareness of the potential and needs of the target service user group.
- Increased understanding of the service user group issues, for example, it would be very unwise to open a five star day centre for D/deaf service users when what they want, and need, is employment.
- Direct contact with service users in a collaborative venture is likely to lead to a deeper understanding of the service users' issues and views.
- Helps to ensure that any end product doesn't merely reflect professional or academic considerations but is grounded in the reality of those who regularly navigate the health and social care system (Clark et al., 2005).
- Working with service users can be very energizing and great fun (McLaughlin, 2005). This can be very stimulating, creating new synergies and promoting new ways of looking at old problems. The GSSC and SCIE also note that this enthusiasm and commitment is contagious and potentially beneficial to everyone (GSSC and SCIE, 2004).

Costs involving service users in research

We have identified a number of possible benefits of user involvement in research and it is now important to consider some of the costs involving service users in research. Involving service users in research is not a cost neutral situation and those who both champion this approach, and those seeking to use it, need to first consider the implications of their choices both in terms of benefits and costs. It is only by analysing both costs and benefits that we can ascertain when such approaches are justified and under what circumstances.

❖ *Costs to research and service development*

Involving service users in research is often written about as if there were no costs and this is patently not the case. When trying to identify what you thought might be costs you may have identified: time, resources, training, support by others and competing pressures.

- In relation to time and resources Kirby accurately points out:

  > All participatory research projects (whether this is with older adults or young people) need the time and resources to support participation. This is easy to underestimate. (Kirby, 2004: 12)

  Service user researchers may well be able to identify research questions or help to ensure the relevance of research, but this is not possible until the co-researchers are recruited. This is not a time resource or cost neutral activity. There are now a number of service user trained research groups who can be commissioned to undertake this work; for example SURF (Service Users Reaching Forward) and SUTRA (Service Users Training and Research Association), but depending on the project, the geographical location or the service user group, the lead researcher may need to recruit members individually – and this will require time and effort.
- Once recruited, the potential service user researchers will also need training to undertake the tasks required within the research project. Lockey et al. (2004) identified that training was not readily available but where it was available it was research project specific. This may create difficulties, because there are no short cuts in service user researcher training, as poor quality training is likely to lead to poor quality research.
- Service user researchers, like people with learning disabilities, physical disabilities or young people, will also need the support of others to be able to undertake the research (McClimens et al., 2007; McLaughlin, 2005; Williams and England, 2005). Again, this support can be resource intensive, as it may include ensuring that service user researchers are transported to research events, undertaking or supporting the completion of practical tasks, acting as a mentor or coach and has led Chappell to comment:

  > If people with learning difficulties need non-disabled allies in the research process in order to convey their experiences in a way which is acceptable to the research community and its gatekeepers, how can the integrity of their accounts be maintained? (Chappel, 2000: 41)

- Patience, things will not necessarily happen quickly; relationships take time to build and changes may not appear dramatic, a long-term perspective is required (Nolan et al., 2007b).
- Poor research experience for service user researchers can have a negative impact on future potential research projects within that service user community. If the experience is negative this is likely to have ramifications beyond the research project whereby service users will be less likely to become

involved in research in the future, thereby contaminating the field for future research.

❖ Costs to service user researchers

Having identified some of the costs to the research and service development involving service users in research, we now move on to issues concerned with service user researchers. In particular, issues of lost opportunities, highlighting of inadequacies, and loss of self-esteem and confidence are highlighted. This is to reinforce that involving service users in research is not a cost neutral activity only in terms of resources but also in terms of its potential impact upon those who participate in the process. There is no rule to say that all participative processes will be experienced positively.

- This point relates to the last point but is seen from a service user researcher's perspective. If a service user researcher decides to use their time to become involved in research they cannot have this time over again to undertake some other activity. Whereas for some it may represent rescue from having to 'fill in time' (Leamy and Clough, 2006: 120) for many others it means curtailing their opportunities for meeting friends, working or searching for work. Deciding to be involved in a research activity is about balancing priorities and if the experience is less than positive service users will be less likely to become involved in research in the future and are likely to pass this message on to friends and colleagues.
- Again, this point relates to situations where academic researchers involve service users in research and do it in such a way that the service users experience a negative exclusionary process. A User Focus Monitoring Group (2005), a mental health project involving service users in research, describe a difficult research experience from the outset:

  > It appeared that the voluntary sector along with the university had decided how the project should be run. It soon became apparent that the non-service users there wanted to run the show. Many of us felt that we were just being used to rubber stamp the process and that we were not true partners in the project. We felt our input was not really wanted. It was a very demoralizing experience as we were regarded as ill and incapable. (A User Focus Monitoring Group, 2005: 41)

- Exclusion may be done wittingly or unwittingly. Unwittingly, the language of the research or written materials acts as a means of segregating service users from professionals and researchers. Research processes that emphasize inadequacies as opposed to abilities are likely to be experienced as prohibitive and as reinforcing negative stereotypes, resulting in a loss of self-esteem or confidence. Thus, volunteering to become a service user researcher can result in a negative outcome.

❖ Costs to academic researchers

- As already noted, involving service users in research is time and resource intensive and may require a trade-off between finishing the research promptly and delivering a quality product. Extra time and resources need to be built into a project involving service user researchers as these are often underestimated. McClimens et al. (2007: 119) also recommend keeping 'a photograph of your loved ones nearby; it may be the only time you see them!'
- Similarly, this will have a knock-on impact to outputs. If outputs take longer and service user researchers are recognized appropriately within any publication (see Chapter 6) this could detract from an academic research assessment exercise which favours single authored publications in international peer reviewed journals.
- Just by bringing academics and service users into close proximity to work on a joint project does not ensure that both sides will necessarily develop an increased or deeper understanding of service user issues. This relies on both sides being open to these possibilities and requires extra facilitation skills of researchers that are not always apparent. A poor experience can result in an academic researcher believing that research of this type is not worth the investment and the development of a negative attitude towards participative research.
- Navigating ethical approval is likely to be more complex, especially where the researcher wishes to involve vulnerable service users in the process.
- Potential limitation in research methods and data analysis. Service user researchers are unlikely to be proficient in advanced qualitative and quantitative research approaches. Thus, if the researcher wishes to involve the service user researchers in all aspects of the research this will restrict the techniques and data analysis strategies that can be implemented.
- Whilst research like this can be fun it can also be very frustrating and challenging. This type of research does not suit everyone.

All these possibilities, with their extra demands and resource constraints, can result in research projects lasting longer and costing more, all of which may impact negatively on an academic researcher's career.

Benefits and costs reconsidered

It is neither possible nor desirable to merely add up the benefits and costs as if they were an arithmetic equation. This is not the case and some benefits and costs will be of greater impact than others, but it is important to try to identify the risks involved in any research approach before beginning. To believe that involving service users in research will of it itself automatically result in better research is as misguided as believing that academically qualified researchers are the only ones who can undertake research. If such research is undertaken poorly or tokenistically it can result in more harm than good. In such circumstances it must be questioned whether the research should have been allowed to progress in the first place.

In considering the appropriateness of involving service users as co-researchers:

The decision is as much a political and ethical one as it is a practical and resource driven one. (McLaughlin, 2006: 1408)

Reflexive Questions

* Thinking about what you have read so far and considering your own personal position, are you in favour of involving service users as co-researchers or not? Why have you come to this decision? What are the implications of your decision for involving service users as co-researchers?

The author has previously argued (McLaughlin, 2007a) that it is important for researchers to be clear and upfront about their views on research matters to allow those reading what they have written to be able to interpret how the author situates themselves and whether they agree with this or not. The author's own position is that he is committed to service users being meaningfully involved in research. This goes back to my practice as a social worker where I sought (not always successfully) to work in partnership against a background of ambiguity and contradiction. My experience of involving service users in research is that they have offered me as much as I have offered them, both personally and in terms of the research project and its outputs. This is both a political and a pragmatic statement in that I believe that involving service users as co-researchers is part of a participation agenda to involve those who are often excluded or treated as the objects of research. Pragmatically, failing to involve service users in research that affects them is to pass up an opportunity to learn about the knowledge that service users have of themselves. In other words, failing to take up this opportunity is to ensure an incomplete picture and to have ignored the possibility of improving the nature and quality of the research. However, this is mediated by the knowledge that involving service users in research must be done both with integrity and due diligence or it can, and does, cause as much harm as good to all involved.

Summary

This chapter has covered the mandate for involving service users as co-researchers. In particular we have highlighted some of the reasons why service users may bother getting involved in research. It was important to identify the expectations service users may have of research and its outcomes. We then examined different levels of service user involvement: tokenism, consultation, collaboration and service user-controlled research. We noted that any research project may include different levels of involvement at different stages of the project and between different service users within the project. Having established what we meant by involvement, we identified benefits and costs for the research project, service user researchers and the non-service user researchers, clarifying a mandate for service user involvement based on positives and advantages that service users may bring to a research project, but also sounding a warning note not to over expect and identifying the importance of proper preparation and support. Finally you were asked to identify where you stood in relation to involving service users in research and how that might impact on how you participated in the journey contained within this book.

Recommended reading

Hanley, B., Bradburn, J., Barnes, M., Evans, C., Goodare, H., Kelson, M., Oliver, S., Thomas, S., and Wallcraft, J. (2004) *Involving the Public in Health and Social Care Research: Briefing Notes for Researchers*, Eastleigh: Involve. This is a highly accessible document advocating service user involvement in research. This paper can also be accessed via the *INVOLVE* website (www.invo.org.uk) which contains many publications that can be read online or downloaded in relation to service user involvement in health and social care research.

Lowes, L. and Hulat, I. (eds) (2005) *Involving Service Users in Health and Social Care Research*, London: Routledge. This collection of articles provides both theoretical and practical examples of service user research involvement in a range of service areas.

Nolan, M., Hanson, E., Grant, G. and Keady, J. (eds) (2007) *User Participation in Health and Social Care Research: Voices, Values and Evaluation*, Maidenhead, Open University Press. A collection of care case studies reflecting a diverse approach to involving service users highlighting both strengths and weaknesses.

3 Ethical Issues in Involving Service Users in Research

Introduction

This chapter examines the often overlooked ethical issues concerned in involving service users in research. Whilst the government, regulatory bodies, professionals and service users have all supported the involvement of service users in research few writers have paid much attention to the ethical issues identified by this approach and their implications for practice. Ethical issues are important in any research; as we have already seen, research is neither intrinsically neutral nor inherently beneficial. In recent years the UK has witnessed the scandal of babies' organs being retained for research at Alder Hey Hospital without their parents' knowledge or consent. This was only the last in a series of health related ethically suspect research studies which have included the non-treatment of syphilis in the Tuskagee Syphilis Study (Brandt, 1978), the non-treatment of a pre-cancer symptomatic group of women in New Zealand (Smith, 1999), and the public funding by America in Asian, African and Caribbean countries to test AZT, an antiviral HIV drug against placebos (Plomer, 2005). All of these studies adopted a scientific approach to charting the progress of the individual diseases to their conclusion, the death of the research subjects. The researchers in all these studies, and in the Alder Hey case, could argue that their research increased our medical knowledge of the different diseases and in so doing helped us to develop more effective treatments. This is a utilitarian position often summed up by the phrase, 'the greatest good of the greatest number' or 'the greatest quantity of pleasure with the smallest quantity of pain' (McIntyre, 1987). Utilitarianism, which is usually associated with Bentham, is a normative theory which identifies a particular standard for guiding and appraising behaviour. Actions can then be judged solely by their effects on human welfare and that if the pain of a few can be outweighed by the pleasure of many that action is then acceptable. Thus, it could be argued that the suffering of a few people with syphilis, cancer, HIV/aids or to have their babies' organs retained for research, is justified in that many will benefit from their sacrifice. The sacrifice of the few is justified by the good they achieve for everyone else. For utilitarianism there is no reason in principle why the greater gains of some should not compensate for the pain of a few. Utilitarianism allows researchers, and others, to treat other human beings as means to an end and not as ends in themselves. Treating others as means, or objects, results in the legitimation of a moral calculus whereby some people's life chances can be overridden for the increased life chances of others. This begs the question of who is to decide whose life chances are to be sacrificed for the greater good of the many. This directs us to questions of power. The Tuskagee Indians were not a powerful group within American society. Plomer (2005) points out that the antiviral HIV trials in Asian, African and Caribbean countries were conducted under ethical standards that would not have been accepted within the US and resulted in the death of several thousand children needlessly. This, Plomer (2005) suggests, demonstrates that the funder, the Department of Health and Human Services, a US public funding body, was willing to routinely provide life saving drugs to Americans whilst denying them to thousands of citizens in the developing or majority world. In so doing the US was conveying the message that their government placed less value on the lives of non-Americans and were willing to sacrifice such nations to benefit Americans.

These examples from biomedical research are important, but those of us who work in other areas of health and social care should not be complacent as there are plenty of non-biomedical examples. Homan (1991) cites Humphrey's study of the homosexual behaviour in men's public toilets in the USA, otherwise known as the 'tearoom trade', as one of the most unethical methodologies in the history of social research. More will be said about this later.

In response to such behaviours many professions have developed their own ethical codes of behaviour.

Reflexive Questions

✳ If you were to devise an ethical code for involving service users in research, what would you include within the code? Does your profession have an ethical code? Are there any elements from it you would like to include or exclude in your code?

Butler (2002) makes the observation that when professional groups claim their own distinctive ethical code they are in fact making a claim for a disciplinary or occupational distinctiveness.

> Social work research is about social workers, what they think, what they believe, what knowledge they claim and what they do with it, and its primary (but not only) audience will be social workers, service users and those who determine who falls into which category for the purposes of public policy. (Butler, 2002: 241)

You could quite easily substitute nursing, midwifery, podiatry, occupational therapy or rehabilitation officers or any other health and social care professional group for social workers. The point here is that many health and social care professions have their own ethical codes which, although similar, are not similar enough to be included in just one health and social care code. Each of the professions would argue that their code signifies the special nature, or unique selling point, of their professional grouping which marks them apart from others. Such claims are both a claim for professional competence and a desire to stake out an area of knowledge and distinctiveness for their professional group.

In trying to generalize from the different codes there are a number of common principles within the health and social care literature derived from biomedical ethics relating to: respect for autonomy, beneficence, non-maleficence, justice and scope (Beauchamp and Childress, 1989). 'Respect for autonomy' refers to the need to treat others as ends in themselves and not simply as means. In other words, we should respect the autonomy of each individual as long as that is congruent with respecting the autonomy of others. As Butler (2002) identified, this principle predicts, amongst other things, the need to obtain informed consent and to preserve confidentiality whilst barring wilful deceit or deception.

'Beneficence' and 'non-maleficence', translates more commonly to 'doing good' and 'not doing harm'. Within a medical context this can be reduced to a rational calculation whereby the treatment will result in a net benefit for patients.

> In an ideal world, no research would involve any risk or harm to anyone involved – but in health care, this is unrealistic. We have to accept that some of what we do as nurses may cause immediate harm, balanced by a more important long-term benefit (such as giving a painful injection of medication). Similarly, people who are research subjects may benefit directly from research interventions, but for many the benefits are less immediate, and they may need to be made aware of the future benefits of others. (Johnson et al., 2004: 9)

As can be seen from the above, guidance to nurses from the Royal College of Nursing research may be experienced as directly painful or harmful and that the benefits may not be immediately recognizable and may in fact benefit others more than them. In the RCN's revised guidance Haigh et al. (2007) note that all research is potentially harmful, not just invasive procedures but also naturalistic enquiries into sensitive topics which can result in emotional distress and potential harm. Thus, for health and social care research, reducing the risk of harm is essential and that a cost–benefit analysis is undertaken indicating that the benefits will outweigh the harm.

'Justice' refers to the moral requirement to deal fairly with competing claims and thus prohibits pursuing one's own interests at the cost of others' legitimate interests; misusing scarce resources or favouring one's own community of interest at the expense of others. In combination, certain other moral principles may be derived and of particular interest to us is Butler's (2002) identification of Gillon's (1994: 186) combination of beneficence and respect for autonomy, which proposes that it is not enough just to respect autonomy but that there is a moral duty to act in such a way as to increase autonomy and thus to promote empowerment.

The 'scope' or application of these ethical principles represents the space in which the researcher can act in response to their own moral conscience. This is the arena in which the researcher can decide which principle should take precedence if there is a conflict. As such, it is clear that these four principles and scope do not remove the need for researchers to engage with moral issues but provide an architecture in which to engage with the complexities and ambiguities of research. To this end Husband's notion of the 'morally active practitioner' can be translated into the need to develop the 'morally active researcher' who would:

> Recognise the implementation of professional ethical guidelines as desirable and as being permanently irreducible to routine ... Morally engaged practitioners (*researchers*) could not hide within professional ethical anaesthesia, but would retain their responsibility for their professional practice and its implications. (Husband, 1995: 87; researchers added to original quote)

It is the position of this author that the rote implementation of ethical codes, however high principled and well meaning, is no substitute for researchers exercising their own ethical integrity as morally active researchers. The morally active researcher accepts the infrastructure provided by an ethical code but realizes that ethical codes cannot, and could not, predict every situation that a researcher will experience. Accepting this, the morally active researcher expects to, and is willing to grapple with, the implications of the nuances, decisions and non-decisions, planned and unplanned consequences that make up the reality of research.

Reflexive Questions

✳ Thinking about research ethics, can you identify any ethical differences between involving service users as co-researchers as opposed to using academic research assistants in this role? This is a topic we will review at the end of this chapter; you may want to write down your answer now to review then.

We have identified why there is a need for ethical research given the abuses of researchers in the past, the potential for harm of research and the need to avoid abuse in the present and the future. We have also identified that whilst ethical codes provide a direction of travel, they do not absolve the researcher from having to engage with the ethical nature of their research and the need to adopt a morally active research approach. This is a subject we will return to in relation to research ethics committees.

In order to explore the ethical challenges of working with service users as co-researchers the next part of this chapter is structured into three key sections; the issues prior to the start of the research, ethical issues during the research and ethical issues following the collection and analysis of the data. This is a false continuum in many ways, as one section can easily run into another and it should not be thought that some of the issues faced prior to the start of the process will also not be revisited during or at the end of the research, but for conceptual ease this linear process will be used, accepting that research is often more circular and messier than described here.

Ethical issues prior to the research commencing

It is not always as easy as it may appear to decide when a research study is conceived, but in relation to this section it is considered the research has begun when the interview schedule is started, the literature review undertaken or questionnaires sent out. There are a number of issues that need to be considered and these include who decides on the area of study, who funds the research, the need to obtain ethical and research governance approval before the research begins, informed consent including the use of covert methods, recruitment of service user co-researchers and reward and recognition of service user co-researchers.

❖ *Who decides what research to undertake?*

Who decides what is researched can come from a number of sources. This may include funding from the national research councils like the Economics and Social Research Council (ESRC) or the Medical Research Council (MRC), by competitive tendering from government departments like Department of Health or Department for Children, Schools and Families; related organizations like Skills for Health and Skills for Care; research funded by the large philanthropic organizations like the Joseph Rowntree Foundation, Nuffield Foundation or Leverhulme Trust Foundation. There is also research commissioned by area health authorities, local authority departments, charities or the private health and social care providers which tend to focus on particular issues like personalized care, care planning or minimum support units for people with disabilities. Research is also funded by private companies, like drug companies, who are set to benefit financially from the research results and these may raise ethical concerns. For example, in the author's opinion, it is unethical to accept research funds from organizations that engage in torture, produce their goods in 'sweatshops' abroad or engage in pornographic productions. Besides the difficulties of knowing whether any of these activities are actually being undertaken the funding becomes even more problematic when we consider whether research funding should be accepted from tobacco companies, baby milk manufacturers or fast food chains who may perceive the funding as an opportunity to launder their public image (Alderson, 1955). These types of funding raise ethical issues that need to be considered and different research projects may reach different decisions as to whether they would accept or apply for such funding. This is not to say that any one group is right or wrong but to suggest that any researcher needs to make a reasoned and informed ethical decision as to whom they will apply to, or from whom they will accept funding. Ideally this should be done with the service user co-researchers. This is not always possible, however, as until any money is secured service user co-researchers may not be identified or, if they are, they may be understandably unwilling to take part in the process. In reading the literature on research governance it could be argued that involving service users at the pre-research stage before the funding and research bid is decided is unethical and that ethical committee approval should be obtained before any researcher talks to potential service user co-researchers. If this is the case it is important that the funding source is discussed with service user co-researchers at the first opportunity so that any potential service user co-researcher who is unhappy with the source of funding can leave the project.

❖ Research governance and ethics committees

Once the funding has been secured and a research strategy completed ethical approval will be required before the research can commence. Ethical research committees are well established in the NHS and universities but social care has only more recently begun to establish accountability frameworks for ethical governance approval. Ethics and research governance committees have the power and responsibility to veto an application when it is unethical, would do harm or requires further development. They are also required to consider whether the research can be deemed as worthwhile, whether it makes an original contribution to knowledge and whether it is likely to benefit patients, service users, carers or their families directly or indirectly. Importantly, this raises an issue for students of the health and social care for whom it is no longer sufficient reason to undertake empirical research for the sole purpose of research training as these ethical requirements demand that the research should be more than a repetition of a previous study but must also meet other criteria in terms of 'worthwhileness', originality and being of benefit to others. This raises the challenge as to how do we decide 'worthwhileness' and 'worthwhileness' to whom? These are separate questions as is the question as to whose interests are paramount when there is a conflict in terms of 'worthwhileness'.

In 2001 The Department of Health published the *Research Governance Framework for Health and Social Care* (Department of Health, 2001a) requiring local authorities, for the first time, to establish a research ethics governance framework. Prior to this researchers would contact local authorities and ask for senior management approval to conduct research within their authority. This earlier system was dependent on who the senior manager was and their understanding of research and the need for ethical approval.

The Research Governance Framework (RGF) was established to protect research participants from the risks associated with research and two of its five domains are of particular interest to us, namely ethics and health and safety. The ethical domain of the research governance framework is focused on ensuring that the dignity, rights, safety and well-being of actual or potential research participants are protected. For collaborative research this requirement should also be considered as a requirement for the service user co-researchers as well as research respondents. In other words, service user involvement in research demands a double standard. This double standard not only requires lead researchers to ensure the dignity, rights and well-being of research participants but also co-researchers. It is surely unethical to consider protecting the dignity, rights and well-being of research participants without also providing the same level of protection and concern for those with whom one is working, or vice versa. The same is also true for the health and safety domain where the researcher is responsible for the safety of research participants and co-researchers. These requirements provide an extra ethical dimension for collaborative research, potentially making it more complex and challenging. It is also worth noting that co-researchers' and research respondents' interests may not always be co-terminus and a decision may need to be taken to foreshorten an interview or research activity where either the research respondent's or co-researcher's dignity, rights, well being or safety are in danger of becoming compromised.

The Health Service was much quicker to respond to the RGF establishing local research ethics committees (LREC) in each geographical area. These committees are formed of voluntary members, of whom one-third are lay members, that is they are not employed in health care related posts. They will though, all be users or potential users of the health service either for themselves or their families. The rest of the committee is made up of medical, educational and scientific experience and expertise. Each committee is supported by a local administrator and the NHS National Research Ethics Service (NRES) (www.nres.org.uk) which, amongst other things, provides an electronic downloadable research ethics application form.

Provided that any research proposal is not a clinical trial of a new medical product it can be assessed by the local research ethics committee. If it is a multi-site application whose remit falls within one area that is the responsibility of one body or organization then it can be considered by any LREC in that area. However, if it is a multi-sited application spanning two different areas then applicants may need to submit to both geographical local research ethics committees. If the application covers more than two separate geographical areas the application should be submitted to a Multi-Centred Ethics Committee (Haigh, 2007).

Within social care the introduction and implementation of the RGF occurred when children and families and adult services were being split. Children and families work was being relocated beside education and coming under the responsibility of the Department for Children, Schools and Families as opposed to the Department of Health. This has resulted in patchy implementation of the RGF, with it generally being fully implemented within adult services but not so in children's services. In fact some local authorities known to the author have stated that they do not intend implementing the RGF within children services until the Department for Children, Schools and Families (DCSF) tells them to do so! At the other end of the spectrum there are a number of local authorities who have used the RGF as an opportunity to develop a more corporate ethical governance framework including other aspects of local authority services. In recognition of this unsatisfactory situation and the 'diverse nature and fragile research infrastructure' of social care (DH et al., 2008: 1) the Department of Health published joint guidance in 2008 (DH et al., 2008) with the DCSF, Association of Directors of Adult Social Services (ADASS) and the Social Services Research Group. However, it should be noted that this is draft guidance, the ADASS has not yet approved the document in full, the DCSF, whilst wishing to promote the guidance, is intending to develop is own guidance for all those working with children, and the guidance does not cover voluntary or private social care providers who are researching their own provision, which has not been commissioned or referred by the NHS or local authorities. Whilst this document is to be welcomed for its recognition of the distinctive nature of social care research governance requirements it still provides no mandatory cover for children, who are often seen as the most vulnerable group in practice and where pubic scandals have driven policy and practice (Butler and Drakeford, 2003). It will also be interesting to observe how ethical research frameworks develop within Children's Trusts which will contain both local authority and NHS personnel.

Ethics and research governance committees have the power and responsibility to veto applications where the committee deem the research to be unethical, where the researcher does not have the skills or abilities to carry out the research, where the research could do harm or where the research proposal is insufficiently developed. Haigh (2007: 130) has identified a range of reasons why ethical permission may be withheld:

- Lack of clear research question.
- Vague, unclear or unscientific methodology.
- No clear understanding of research philosophies selected.
- Lack of statistical advice.
- Sample size (too large or too small).
- Lack of peer review.
- Non-inclusion of the research tools to be used (questionnaire/interview schedule).
- Lack of consideration for research participants.
- Lack of support mechanisms if participants become upset.
- Poorly constructed participant information sheet (Haigh, 2007).

Haigh (2007: 130–1) also admits that research committees in health are more likely to act favourably towards a quantitative research proposal and that qualitative approaches will have a more difficult time. This raises particular difficulties for research involving service users as researchers as this is more likely to be located within a qualitative paradigm (see Chapter 5). It is also likely that such research would want to involve the co-researchers in the development of the research tools and development of information sheets, requiring committees to accept a degree of risk they may not be used to. Research ethics committees will generally try and respond to an application for research approval within 60 days, but it is wise to consider building in more time than this to allow for answering any research ethics committee questions which are likely to arise until this type of research becomes mainstreamed.

Depending on the research project, e.g. a project on the mental health of children looked after, you may need to get approval of both the LREC and the local authority's research ethics committee. If the researcher is located within a university they will also have to get approval from the university's ethics committee. All this can result in delays and runs the danger whereby each committee will request changes that are contradictory. Also, LRECs have been viewed as unsympathetic to social care researchers and qualitative approaches. In a Department of Health's update on the implementation of the research governance framework they noted that:

> Some experienced researchers working in the field of social care reported that the process of approval by NHS Research Ethics Committees was often frustrating and time-consuming (Tinker, 2001). Common complaints about the NHS REC's includes their focus on research methods rather than ethical issues, the lack of expertise

in social science methods, the burden of paperwork in making applications, and lengthy delays which can be catastrophic for short term projects. (Department of Health, 2007b: 4)

This has also led to critics like Furedi (2002) to view such committees highly critically and negatively, as bureaucratic gatekeepers overly concerned with protective paternalism and using ethics as the new managerial ideology for controlling which types of research methodologies get approved and in which research areas.

The process of research governance has become more complex with the introduction in England and Wales of the Mental Capacity Act (2005) which although primarily not about research does provide (sections 30–4) a statutory framework and provisions for the involvement of people who lack capacity to consent to their involvement in 'intrusive' research. In particular the Act highlights the position of people with learning difficulties, illnesses such as dementia or Alzheimer's and those with mental health problems. 'Intrusive' is defined as research that would normally require the consent of a person with capacity in order for the research to be lawful. This would suggest that all research involving service users as respondents or co-researchers is likely to be subject to these provisions.

Gaining ethical research approval is a process and not merely an end in itself. As previously noted, it can never be assumed that all ethical considerations will, or could be, identified prior to any research commencing. Hence the need to adopt the stance of a morally active researcher as discussed previously. Doing one's duty and completing the ethical research governance forms is not the same as being morally responsible. Compliance is insufficient; compliance leads to routinized practices, technical efficiency and habituated responses at the cost of denying professional responsibility. Achieving a successful outcome from the research governance and ethics committee is important to the morally active researcher but it is only the beginning of a process that will continue to the end of the research and beyond.

Ethical considerations need to include both those who will be the research subjects and those who will be undertaking the research.

The morally active researcher needs to be continually engaged in reflecting upon the ethical dimensions of the research process, not just for the research participants but also for the collaborative researchers. (McLaughlin, 2007b: 184)

Both groups need to be considered as separate entities and as a dynamic inter-active relationship within the research interview process. Research governance and ethics committees like to know how researchers will ensure that research subjects have given their informed consent to be part of a research study; this is a subject we move to next.

❖ *Informed consent*

Reflexive Questions
✳ If you were asked to participate in a research study what information would you like to know about and what safeguards would you like before you could decide whether you wished to participate or not? Having considered the position of a research subject consider the same issues from the point of view of someone who is being asked to become a service user co-researcher or not. Are there any differences in the two roles, and if so why?

Informed consent implies that the research subject knows the purpose of the study, who the funder is, what their involvement entails, what the level of risk to the subject is (including psychological distress), how their confidentiality and anonymity will be ensured, how they will be identified in any publication and how they will be able to find out the results of the research. Besides, this information good practice assumes that respondents will also be advised that they may decide to end the research process at any time without prejudice. In particular early closure or failure to participate would not affect their right to treatment or services. It is also important that this information is provided in plain language, using cartoons or drawings if appropriate, and in the potential research subject's preferred language. It should also be noted that agreement to participate in a research study at the start of the project is not the same as agreeing to participate once the research has begun or after the research's completion (Thompson, 2002). This is as true for service user co-researchers as it is for research respondents. It may be more helpful to consider informed consent as informing-for-consent (Tymuch, 1997). Informing-for-consent is part of an ongoing process rather than a single event. Such a view also has implications for recruitment and suggests that the lead researcher may need to recruit more co-researchers than they think they may need as people may leave at different points of the process and not return.

Once informed consent is given it needs to be recorded. It is important to record informed consent, because if there is a dispute it will then not be a matter of one person's word against another's. For service user co-researchers this is important as it represents an agreement by the co-researchers of the conditions under which the research project is to be delivered and their part within it. As such, the informed consent agreement works alongside the job description and person specification (see Chapter 5) to ensure that, as far as possible, co-researchers are aware of what they are getting involved in. The record may be written or taped, depending on whatever is appropriate to the situation.

❖ The use of covert methods

In considering informed consent it is important to consider the place of covert methods within service user research. Covert methods usually involve the concealment of the researcher, or service user co-researcher, within an otherwise acceptable social role (Homan, 1991). Covert research methods usually involve some degree of participant observation, but also may make use of modern technology to 'bug', using video, photography, mobile telephones, tape machines or other means of recording situations. As previously mentioned, Homan (1991) cites Humphreys' study of the 'tearoom trade' as an example of the most unethical research ever undertaken. The 'tearooms' in question were men's public toilets in the United States, in which Humpreys acted as 'watchqueen' or lookout, coughing when strangers appeared, thus alerting the men inside who were engaging in sexual activity (Humphreys, 1975). Not only did he observe the events but he recorded the details of the men's age, dress and car registrations through which he was later able to trace them to their home addresses. Then, whilst undertaking a health survey, he included 50 of his own subjects whom he later visited at their homes after changing his dress and hairstyle.

Within service user research there are at least two possible areas for covert methods. First, the researcher could use the service user co-researchers, for example ex-drug users, as cover to gain direct access to drug transactions. Secondly, the lead researcher could use the service user co-researchers to film or record such transactions without the informed consent of the drug dealers or other parties. Homan (1991) identifies 13 arguments why covert research methods should not be used including that they flout the principles of informed consent, erode personal liberty, betray trust, pollute the research environment and are invisibly reactive. Covert methods can thus be seen as highly controversial and problematic. Where covert methods have been used there has often been a claim that the end justifies the means. This is a highly contentious argument as it begs the question as to who is to decide that the needs of one group should be subservient to the needs of another. This also takes us back to the start of this chapter when we identified some of the abuses of research and the rationale for an ethical research practice. Most research codes prohibit covert research and the deceit which is inherent within it, but contain a rider that such research could be justified in an exceptional case. Butler (2002) provides such a rider in the ethical code for social work and social care research when he proposes that three conditions should be satisfied before deception or concealment could be considered as justified.

> Only in cases where no alternative strategy is feasible, where no harm to the research subject can be foreseen and where the greater good is self-evidently served, are procedures involving the deception or concealment permissible for social work and social care researchers. (point 9: 246)

Any service user research project considering the use of covert methods needs to seriously consider their research approach and can expect a significant challenge from the ethics and research governance committees and from their peers if the research should ever reach the public arena.

❖ Anonymity and confidentiality

Confidentiality and anonymity are sometimes confused. Anonymity refers to preserving the identity of the research participants to only those within the research team. This can become compromised where participation is secured through a third party, e.g. a head of service or if the service user co-researchers are asked to identify other possible service users as research respondents. In these situations absolute guarantees are not possible and potential research respondents should be honestly advised of who will know they have participated. Confidentiality, on the other hand, refers to ensuring that the attributions of comments or opinions in reports, articles, books or other media cannot be linked to individual participants. This includes both direct attribution, where the name of the respondent is identified and indirect attribution, where attribution may be deduced from a collection of characteristics or role descriptors make it possible to identify an individual. In such circumstances any reports may need to consider restricting or changing the amount of contextual detail to avoid potential identification of an individual or small group.

❖ Groundrules

Good practice would suggest that groundrules should be developed with co-researchers, but it may be worth considering whether it is helpful identifying which, if any, of the groundrules are non-negotiable. The job description and person specification also provides a potentially mixed message to potential participants. On the one hand potential service user researchers may be pleased that the lead researcher has given thought as to how service users may be involved in the research, whilst on the other hand they may feel constrained that there is no room for negotiation. Lead researchers need to consider how specific their job description and person specification should be and to include points which identify opportunities for influencing the research direction, for example, 'developing research questions' and 'participating in data analysis', in the example above.

❖ *Reward and recognition*

Reward and recognition covers both the reimbursement of expenses and payment for the skills, expertise and time that service user co-researchers contribute to a research project. Expenses need to be paid and should be paid as soon as possible after the expense has been incurred. In certain situations it may even be desirable for these to be paid before rather than after they have been incurred. It may well be all right for professional researchers to wait for their expenses to be paid as part of their monthly wage, but this is not the same for those who may be dependent on benefits. In these cases the money is likely needed to be managed very tightly and any disturbance may result in a meal to be missed or a trip out to be cancelled. These expenses may need to be higher than normal to cover extra costs, such as a personal assistant, the need for specialized transport, stationery, equipment, accommodation, child care or caring responsibilities.

Reflexive Questions

✳ The payment of expenses is uncontroversial, whereas there has been more debate about paying co-researchers for their time and expertise as co-researchers. What is your position on this point? Why should we pay service user co-researchers? Are there any disadvantages in paying co-researchers?

There are a number of reasons why we should consider paying service user co-researchers and Steel (2006) identifies those listed below:

- As an incentive to become actively involved in a research project.
- To allow a broader range of people to be involved in the research.
- To support equity of power in research partnerships.
- To support inclusion. By offering payments, people who are usually excluded may be able to get involved and make a contribution to the research affecting them.

- It can directly lead to a more effective and equitable involvement of people who use services by easing the financial constraints.
- It helps to reduce barriers to involvement.
- To clarify expectations and responsibilities of service user co-researchers.

The above provides a compelling case for paying service user co-researchers for their time, expertise and skills just as we would any other researcher.

> People who use services should be paid for their time and expertise to a level consistent with other members of the research team. This will depend on a variety of factors and circumstances. For example, it's unfair to expect people who are unpaid to sit alongside paid non-executive members of research advisory groups or committees, or to ask them to give their time for free when others are paid for their time as part of their day job, or through locum fees. On the other hand, where a committee/group is entirely voluntary, payment for time cannot reasonably be expected. (Steel, 2006: 5)

There are, however some further considerations that need to be borne in mind. Whenever payment enters the equation it may subtly change the relationship between the researcher and co-researcher, making it a more formal relationship. It also allows the lead researcher to hold the co-researchers to account and provides an arena in which dissatisfactions between co-researchers may be played out where one co-researcher may feel another is not pulling their weight and is being paid the same amount as they are. Such human resource issues are common in all organizations and will need to be handled sensitively and firmly by the lead researcher. In terms of payments the lead researcher will also need to consider whether there is a lump sum payment for participation, payment in relation to expertise, payment in relation to the time spent or the tasks undertaken or some combination of these. Whichever method is chosen it should be transparent and discussed with the co-researchers before they agree to be part of the project. It should however, not be assumed that paying co-researchers will automatically result in the independence of their views being compromised. We would not say the same about paying academic researchers and there is no evidence to suggest that service user co-researchers are any less ethically oriented.

In such situations it is also important to consider employment law, national insurance, tax, state benefits and allowances, as these may all be affected by payment. It may also occur that someone may not wish to be paid because of the fear of losing a benefit or allowance. Turner and Beresford (2005b) in a report for SCIE identified that there was increasing tension between service users getting involved with their communities, as the government would wish, and the day-to-day workings of the state benefits system. In particular they highlighted that the rules for payment were unclear; people were concerned that if they were paid they were breaking the law, some were worried that if they were paid they would lose their benefits, whilst others worried they would have to start paying tax. The Department of Health are aware of this as a problem and have published a guide for service providers, service users and carers to help them identify any consequences of receiving payments for engaging in research activities (Department of Health, 2006). It is important that whatever system is used that it should be legal, that service users should have the choice of being paid, that service user co-researchers should not exploited but rewarded commensurate with their input, and that they should not be financially worse off by contributing to a research project.

Ethical issues during the research

In this phase service user co-researchers are likely to have their closest contact with those who are being researched. In particular, this section will consider the need for support of service user co-researchers, research subjects, the storing of data and the voluntary nature of research.

❖ Support for service user co-researchers

In this period of the research contact and interaction between service users and service user co-researchers there are likely to be both anticipated and unanticipated ethical issues. It is possible that service users who have physical disabilities, people with learning disabilities or who have suffered a sudden infant death (or been subject to all three) may require support during this phase. Within any ethical approval form it is likely that the lead researcher will have identified the importance of providing independent support to research respondents, as the research questions may trigger powerful feelings that will require support following the completion of the interview. In certain cases the research interview may need to be stopped, either temporarily or permanently, if the research respondent becomes very upset. Similarly the topics under investigation, or even the respondent's answers, may trigger feelings that the co-researcher thought they had dealt with. It is thus important to consider both the support needs of co-researchers and the research respondents. It is inappropriate to consider that the lead researcher should undertake this role even if they are registered nurses, social workers or counsellors. To do so would be to blur boundaries and confuse roles; it is, however, their responsibility to ensure an appropriate support strategy is in place. If possible, it is best to provide this support from a different source so that both research respondents and service user co-researchers may know that they have their own support channel which is not 'contaminated' by the other.

During the research the lead researcher should also be sensitive to the needs of both service user co-researcher's and respondent's discomfort. It may also be appropriate to check that both are willing to carry on. Respondents' levels of discomfort may be reduced when they are permitted to be accompanied by a trusted friend, for co-researchers it may also be necessary to consider the need for a co-researcher to be accompanied by another co-researcher. In making such a decision the lead researcher needs to be aware of their duty of care to protect both the respondents and the service user co-researchers. In certain situations this may have a negative effect upon the research, but it is clear that the health and safety of research respondents and co-researchers should take precedence.

❖ *Storage of research data*

At this stage of the process the issues of data recording and storage should have been considered and agreed previously. It is important that any written, taped, drawn, photographed or videoed data is stored safely. It is part of the service user co-researcher's responsibility, along with the lead researcher to ensure research respondents are aware of what data is being collected, why it is being collected, how it will be used, how it will be stored and how long it will be stored for, and importantly what are the arrangements for its safe disposal. If such data is not stored securely it would breach the research respondent's right to anonymity and confidentiality. This is particularly important when you are dealing with sensitive information that could be misused by third parties.

Alongside this it is essential within this phase of the process to re-iterate the importance of confidentiality. A research project can be a very exciting time for lead researchers and service user co-researchers alike, but it is imperative that service user co-researchers do not decide to share their research data and 'stories' with their friends at the local club or pub. Whilst this desire is understandable, it is unethical. This may also refer to carers who may wish to know what the service user co-researcher has been up to whilst they were engaged in the research project. If the service user co-researcher is unable to abide by these rules they may need to be asked to leave the project to protect the research respondents. This is the type of anticipated issue that should have been discussed as part of the training programme with an agreed process for dealing with alleged lapses of ethical conduct.

❖ *Voluntary involvement*

In relation to informed consent we identified the importance of being clear with any potential research respondent about the nature of the research, their rights to anonymity and confidentiality and their right to withdraw from the process at any point without prejudice. As Oliver (2003) notes, research respondents are acting in a voluntary capacity and have the right to withdraw from the research without giving notice, however frustrating this might be for the research team. Service user co-researchers will also have entered into the research project on a voluntary basis, although subsequently they may have become remunerated to undertake certain research activities. It is important to have identified a process for dealing with service user co-researchers should they decide they no longer wished to be party to the research project to minimize any disruption or damage to the project. In such circumstances it would be helpful to have an agreed protocol, although this is likely to be no more than a moral contract as it is difficult to identify circumstances where a lead researcher would take legal proceedings against a service user co-researcher for breach of contract.

❖ *Respecting the research site*

Researchers need to consider how their involvement in the research project will impact upon the research site. Research sites should be left undisturbed after a research study (Creswell, 2007). In respecting the research site lead researchers and service user co-researchers need to be cognizant of their impact and minimize any disruption on both the physical setting and the lives of the research respondents. This is particularly important if the research is being undertaken on a ward or residential facility, when the researchers may have to consider the timing of their research visits so that they achieve minimal intrusion on the lives of the patients or residents. If the research fails to take due regard of the integrity of the research site they are likely to compromise that site for further research. This will potentially make the service users, and staff who work with them, less likely to engage with future research projects and lead to a negative consideration of all research, thus reducing the potential of research to impact positively in the future.

There is an exception to this rule and this is where the research project is primarily based upon an action research method, where the aim is both to contribute to basic knowledge in the social sciences whilst at the same time seeking to improve a service or situation in everyday life (Coghlan and Bannick, 2001). In these circumstances it is axiomatic that change will happen, but the lead researcher along with the service user co-researchers has a responsibility to seek, as far as is possible, that these changes should be empowering but not oppressive.

Ethical issues following the collection and analysis of the data

Following the collection and analysis of the data ethical issues still need to be considered. In particular this section highlights the ethical issues concerned with the authorship, publication and dissemination of any report and finally the ending of the research project.

❖ Authorship

Ethical codes suggest that all publications from a research project, 'Should properly and in proportion to their contribution acknowledge the part played by all participants' (Butler, 2002: 247). What 'properly' and 'in proportion to their contribution' actually means is more difficult to tie down. Is it reasonable to expect that joint authorship means that the joint author(s) have taken an equal part in the shaping of a project, collection of data, analysis of data and its writing up? Quite clearly joint authorship does not necessarily entail an equal share of the work. This is recognized in universities and in the Research Assessment Exercise (RAE) where jointly authored articles are expected to identify the percentage input of each author. However, this does not answer the question at which percentage is it not reasonable to include someone as a joint author, whilst for two authors a 50:50 split or even a 70:30 split does not seem unreasonable to warrant inclusion – but what about a 90:10 or 95:5 split? Importantly, it should be remembered that quantity and quality are not the same things. Also, as many research projects involving service users may have six or more people involved, any calculations about percentage input will be potentially more complex and more difficult to extrapolate. This is further complicated when service user co-researchers undertake different tasks potentially requiring some measure or comparison of the value of each task. This can become extremely complex and runs the risk of upsetting or demotivating service user co-researchers. It is often easier, and potentially more ethical, to include all participants as joint authors on research reports although the report may identify who undertook which task. Having decided who to include as authors it is also important to consider the order of the names; if there are one or two people who have clearly done more than the others they should come first. Otherwise alphabetical order is often the easiest way to decide.

Whilst this may help to clarify authorship for the main research report, other issues come into force when considering academic articles or other publications that may flow from the research report. The issue of academic articles is particularly pertinent for academically employed researchers whose outputs are primarily measured through their academic output in international peer refereed journals. Roche et al. (2005: 91) note that the production of papers was complicated as they sought to involve the other team members and reached the point where they said:

> We would have benefitted from more time to review articles and smaller numbers of individuals writing each paper.

Seemingly McClimens et al.'s (2007) frustration at taking almost two years to complete a paper is almost palpable. Seeking to involve everyone can have its drawbacks.

Referring back to the principle that acknowledgement of contribution should be in proportion to the contribution, it may be appropriate to identify the service user co-researchers at the end of the article rather than as co-authors. If this is to be the case such authorship issues should be discussed with the service user co-researchers prior to the production of any articles.

❖ Proper names?

When identifying service user co-researchers, whether in the report or subsequent publications, it is important to consider whether service user co-researchers will want their full name, pseudonym or nickname used to identify them. In sensitive areas like HIV, teenage pregnancy or mental health, people may not wish to be able to be identified as living with HIV, being a teenage parent or having a mental health condition. Identification of a service user co-researcher would in these circumstances be alerting others to their condition which they may wish to remain private.

This also raises another related issue, for it is easy to understand why certain service user co-researchers would not wish to be identified; however, what if the lead researcher felt that the research could have a negative impact upon the lives of the co-researchers and they still wished to be identified? Once research is in the public arena, it is by definition open to all and there is no control over who will access it and how they will use it. There is no certainty that it will be used sympathetically or in the way envisaged by the lead researcher and service user co-researchers who may feel embarrassed or hurt by the way it is used by others. It is thus imperative that lead researchers discuss the risks with service user co-researchers prior to publication so that decisions as to how they wish to be acknowledged can be made with the knowledge of potential consequences from · identification and consideration of how to minimize any potential harm.

❖ *Dissemination of research*

Involving service user co-researchers in the dissemination of research at conferences can be a very powerful way of getting a message across. Service user co-researchers can be very effective in making an impact and convincing others of the need for change (Kirby, 2004; Clark et al., 2005). However, it is just as easy for service user co-researchers to be dismissed by professional audiences when little thought has gone into the presentation. Just by involving service user co-researchers in a dissemination event does not necessarily ensure the messages will be heard or that they will have the required impact if there has been little investment in presentation skills. Lead researchers have a responsibility to ensure that service user co-researchers should be trained and supported for any presentations. Also attention needs to be given as to how service user co-researchers wish to be identified to an audience; in extreme cases this may result in the use of false names, speaking from a darkened part of a stage or behind a screen or using modern technology to mask a voice to avoid identification.

❖ *Endings*

Finally, service user co-researchers are likely to have invested a lot of their time, energies and commitment to a research project. For many of these they may have been paid and the end of the research project will signal not only the ending of, we hope, a fruitful experience, but also the end of funding. It is also likely that the research team will have become close through the shared experiences, both planned and unplanned, and the success of completing the project. Ethically it is inappropriate for the research team just to dissolve at the end of the process without any formal acknowledgement of what they have achieved and consideration of what the service user co-researchers could do in the future. It is important to mark the end of a research project properly to allow the members to celebrate the past, their new relationships and to be able to move on to the future. This is significant as service user co-researchers will have developed new skills they may wish to use again and consideration needs to be given as to any other research projects they could join, membership of research review boards or service user organizations where their new skills could be put to use. Lead researchers may move on to new research projects, but this is not as straightforward for service user researchers. Lead researchers also need to consider providing each service user researcher with a transcript or certificate identifying what they did as part of the research, which could then be used as evidence for future employment.

Endings should also consider how the impact or any outcomes from their research will be communicated. As mentioned in Chapter 2, service users who become co-researchers are keen to see that their research has made an impact and it is thus important to identify any ways, if possible, to communicate any changes that occur from their research. This might be done by posting an update on a website, writing to individual members, or any other mutually agreed communication strategy. Whilst it was noted that lead researchers do not have it within their power to ensure any action does result from their research they do need to consider how they can advise their co-researchers if some changes do result from it. This is important in demonstrating that research can make an impact and encourage service user co-researchers to become involved in other research projects as co-researchers or research respondents.

Internet research

This has been treated as a separate section although many of the concerns surrounding the ethics of internet research are identical. However, the Association of Internet Researchers have argued that certain issues are of a different degree when you consider their ethical impact when using the internet (Hewson et al., 2003). This is important as service user co-researchers could be asked to undertake online interviews or focus groups where there are more difficulties in maintaining the participant's privacy, voluntary participation, confidentiality and de-briefing after the research has taken place. In internet research it is much easier for a research respondent to lie about their identity or their age (Hewson et al., 2003). The issue of ensuring you are speaking to genuine service users is very difficult to guarantee. This may be possible where their addresses have been secured from a service user or service provider organization, although this raises sampling issues for consideration in the light of potential possibilities for research respondent dishonesty. In terms of voluntary participation internet research may make this easier with the introduction of a 'withdraw' or 'submit data' button.

For internet-minded researchers the internet provides new opportunities for communication, including email, interactive chat, newsgroups, online questionnaires and the development of a dedicated site for the researchers to share data and data analysis. However, anyone considering the use of the internet as part of their research methodology also needs to consider the risks and the ethical dilemmas provided by research in cyberspace (Haigh and Jones, 2005).

Summary

This chapter has sought to explore the ethical issues concerned with involving service users as co-researchers. The chapter started by highlighting why ethical research was necessary and the development of health and social care professional bodies' research ethical codes. From this we split the ethical process into issues prior to the research began, ethical issues during the research and ethical issues following the collection and analysis of data. In particular, the research ethic and governance framework was highlighted, as was the importance of informed consent, recruitment and training of service user co-researchers, anonymity and confidentiality, reward and recompense, the right to end participation, support for service user co-researchers, storage of data, authorship, dissemination and endings. Earlier in the chapter it was asked whether the issues that affected how we responded to research respondents were the same issues that needed to be considered for service user co-researchers. From what has already been written it should be clear that the issues are the same although the degree is different; for example, we might pay a research respondent for participating in the research is both the same and different as paying a service user co-researcher. Both should be recompensed for their time and experience, although the service user co-researcher is also signing up to a set of expectations which include that they will behave to the same ethical standards as lead researchers.

This chapter also highlighted that the successful research governance and ethical committee approval is not the end point of the ethical process. The research governance and ethical approval process is only a step in the process whose ethical challenges often only appear after committee approval has been obtained. Instead this chapter argues that researchers need to be continually on their guard and to adopt the stance of a morally active researcher.

Recommended reading

Homan, R. (1991) *The Ethics of Social Research*. Harlow: Longmans. A classic text on ethical issues.

Long, T. and Johnson, M. (eds) (2006) *Research Ethics in the Real World: Issues and Solutions for Health and Social Care*. London: Churchill Livingstone, Elsevier. A good introductory text identifying real world ethical problems and their solutions.

Oliver, P. (2003) *The Student's Guide to Research Ethics*. Maidenhead: Open University Press. A good introductory text on key ethical issues for social science students.

4 Knowledge Claims and Service User Research

Introduction

This chapter seeks to identify the knowledge claims made by involving service users in research. In particular the chapter will examine whether the knowledge claims made for involving service users as co-researchers are different from any other type of research or are just the same. The chapter will highlight ontology, epistemology and methodology, standpoint theory and the argument for a different typology of knowledge informed by service user controlled research.

Reflexive Questions

✳ You might like to consider whether you believe there is a difference between researching with service users and the knowledge that will be developed as opposed to researching with non-service user researchers. Will service user researchers use different methods? Will their knowledge claims be any more valid than non-service user researchers. In other words, does service user research create different or better knowledge from that of researching with non-service users? What reasons did you give for your decision?

For as long as can be recalled, we have argued over different ways of knowing. Gods, giants and even reasonable people cannot seem to agree about the nature of reality and how we can understand it. There are – quite simply – different ways of knowing, and students of social science need to be aware of these differences and how they affect the methods they choose to study social phenomena. (Moses and Knutsen, 2007: 1)

Before beginning to unpack the above quote and reflexive question we first need to consider how knowledge claims are traditionally understood and constructed.

Ontology

Three of the core concepts in the philosophy of science are ontology, epistemology and methodology. All three of these concepts are often misunderstood by students and researchers alike and have a tendency to merge together (Crotty, 2003). Ontology is the science or study of being. It is concerned with the nature of existence, 'what is' or beliefs about what there is to know about the world. As Snape and Spencer (2003: 11) note, key ontological questions concern:

- Whether or not social reality exists independently of human conceptions and interpretations.
- Whether there is a common, shared, social reality or just multiple context specific realities.
- Whether or not social behaviour is governed by 'laws' that can be seen as immutable or generalizable.

The first of these points identifies one of the key ontological debates as focusing on whether there is a captive social reality and how it should be constructed. In response to this there are two opposing positions: realism and idealism. Realism posits the view that there is an external reality that exists independently of people's beliefs or understanding about it. In effect reality exists outside the mind. This implies that there is a difference between what the world is and the meaning and interpretation placed upon that world by individuals. Idealism starts from a different perspective and asserts that reality is only knowable through the human mind and through socially constructed meanings (Snape and Spencer, 2003). Idealism asserts that what is real is confined to what is in the mind and consists only of 'ideas'.

These two positions have continuously been discussed and have been modified from their extreme positions. Critical realism (Bhaskar, 1979) and subtle realism (Hammersley, 1992) are variants of realism influenced by idealism, whereby it is accepted there is an external reality which exists independent to our beliefs, understanding and representation, but importantly, reality is only knowable through the human mind and socially constructed representations.

As Crotty (2003: 10) notes in quoting Macquarrie (1973: 57):

If there were no human beings, there might still be galaxies, trees, rocks, and so on – and doubtless there were in those long stretches of time before the evolution of *Homo sapiens* or any other human species that may have existed on earth. (italics in original)

This world will though not have been an intelligible world. Even so, it is conceivable to consider the existence of such a world, and things in that world independent of our consciousness, but that does not imply that meaning exists independent of consciousness. Or, as Crotty so effectively puts it;

> The existence of a world without a mind is conceivable. Meaning without mind is not. (Crotty, 2003: 10–11)

There are similar variations within idealism including subtle idealism and relativism. Subtle idealism recognizes that reality is only knowable through socially constructed meanings but that these meanings are shared, thus creating a collective mind. Whilst relativism also acknowledges that reality is only knowable through socially constructed meanings, but that there is no single reality:

> there can be as many different realities as there are different structures of language and belief. (Hughes and Sharrock, 1997: 145)

So far we have identified different ontological versions of the study of being, or 'what is' the structure of reality or the nature of existence. An underlying ontological issue for us to consider is whether the natural world exists in similar ways to the health and social care world. At the biomedical end of the health perspective there is an obvious link with the natural sciences, but in much of health care and in social work there is a closer affinity to the social world as being very different to the natural world because it is open to subjective interpretation and social construction. This leads us onto discussing the importance of epistemology.

Epistemology

Epistemology refers to 'the nature of knowledge, its possibility, scope and general basis' (Hamlyn, 1995: 242 quoted in Crotty, 2003: 8). Epistemology is thus intimately concerned with what is knowledge. Epistemology seeks to provide a philosophical grounding for knowing and learning about the world and deciding what kinds of knowledge claims are possible and how we can ensure that they are both valid and legitimate. There are a number of competing epistemologies and we will briefly explore four: positivism, constructionism, pragmatism, advocacy/participatory knowledge claims, but it should be noted that none of these typologies is irrefutable.

❖ *Positivist knowledge claims*

Positivism identifies a particular type of relationship between the researcher and the researched which apes the natural sciences and where phenomena are seen as independent of, and unaffected by the behaviour of the researcher. Consequently the researcher can be objective in their research and their investigation be considered as value free. Positivist epistemology thus maintains that meaning exists apart from the operation of the consciousness. That rock in the sea is still a rock. It remains a rock whether anyone is aware of its existence or not. When we recognize it as a rock, we are simply discovering a meaning that was waiting to be discovered. This is similar to the way in which the early ethnographers approached their task. In the objectivist schema understandings and values are considered to be objectified in the people under study and, if we approach our subject in the right way, we can discover the objective truth.

Positivism in very general terms involves the belief that scientific knowledge can be positively verifiable and is thus based on sure and certain foundations and on the discovery of general laws. Delanty (2005) has identified five key tenets of positivism:

- *Scientism or the unity of scientific method* For positivism there is no essential difference between the methods of the natural and the social sciences, both are joined by a unity of method.
- *Naturalism or phenomenalism* Not only is there a unity of method but also a unity in subject matter, the study of reality which is external to the science itself. Positivism entails (a) reductionism or atomism (the view that everything can be reduced to its basic building blocks), (b) a correspondence theory of truth (the view that there is a correspondence between the truths of science and the nature of reality), and (c) phenomenalism or objectivism (the adoption of an objectifying attitude to nature which views nature as existing outside science which can be neutrally observed.
- *Empiricism* Reality consists of what is observable to the senses. Positivism is based on that which is open to observation and verification. The journey from observation to verification follows the experimental method to discover objectively existing general laws from which hypotheses can be drawn to predict what can happen.
- *Value freedom* There is a fundamental distinction between facts and values; science does not make judgments on its subject matter. Science is a neutral activity free of ethical and social values. Values, it is claimed, cannot be derived from facts. Positivism thus involves a commitment to the pursuit of scientific truth, independent of ethical self reflection or personal subjective elements, resulting in scientific knowledge being different from all other

kinds of human knowledge being verifiable and can therefore be held to be universally true.

- *Instrumental knowledge* In general the institution of science as a profession in modern society has favoured the pursuit of technically useful knowledge. (Delanty, 2005)

Thus positivist statements are directly verifiable as true or false by their correspondence with the facts. Social phenomena can be classified, correlated and measured; hypotheses can be formulated and tested, allowing the world to become predictable and with predictability potentially controllable.

Popper (1980) later developed logical positivism or postpositivism high-lighting deductivism or hypothetico-deductivism; logical reasoning in which he contended scientific enquiry can never be accredited with more than provisional acceptance. In this approach knowledge is conjectural (and anti-foundational) – absolute truth can never be established, research is always fallible. Research becomes a process of making knowledge claims and then refining these in relation to the research evidence which will support some and deny others. Research seeks to identify 'true' statements that can help to explain a situation or describe causal relationships. In so doing it is important to adopt an objective approach. Popper's contribution to positivism emphasizes that theory acceptance must always be tentative.

❖ *Constructivist knowledge claims*

Constructivism, in opposition to objectivism and positivism, rejects this objective view of human knowledge. Again constructivism is being used to cover a range of approaches, including interpretivism, modern ethnography, interpretive interactionism and social interactionism, which all share a common view that you cannot research the social world in the same way you research the natural world. Schutz (1978) ably described the difference thus:

> The world of nature, as explored by the natural scientist, does not 'mean' anything to the molecules, atoms and electrons therein. The observational field of the social scientist, however, namely social reality, has a specific meaning and relevance structures for the human beings living, acting and thinking therein. By a series of commonsense constructs they have pre-selected and pre-interpreted this world which they experience as the reality of their everyday lives.(Schutz, 1978: 31)

Human beings are engaged with their world; we are all born into a world of meanings bestowed upon us by our culture and seen through our historical and social lenses (Creswell, 2007). For the constructivist there is no objective truth waiting to be discovered. There is no measurement without meaning. Meaning is constructed, not discovered.

> In this understanding of knowledge, it is clear that different people may construct meaning in different ways, even in relation to the same phenomenon. Isn't this precisely what we find when we move from one era to another or from one culture to another? In this view of things, subject and object emerge as partners in the generation of meaning. (Crotty, 2003: 9)

These meanings though do not exist in the ether waiting to be discovered, but are formed in the interaction with others and through the historical, social and cultural norms that help shape people's lives. Reality cannot be identified apart from the language in which it is embedded. Realities are constructed, re-constructed, interpreted and re-interpreted in and through meanings. Reality in social sciences, and also in the natural sciences, cannot be known independent of the concepts available in language. However, meanings are not totally idiosyncratic – otherwise it would be impossible to communicate. This accepts that there are differences between how service users and non-service users or carers and non-carers experience the world; however, meanings are not finitely specific, meaning is constructed from the interaction between individuals and is related to their historical, cultural and social positions. Disputes about meanings may not necessarily be disputes about the adequacy of our language but may represent inherent features of social reality.

For our purposes we may posit that service users and carers may construct the experience of being nursed or receiving social care differently form others receiving the same service or from those providing the service. This is not to privilege one experience as more authentic, or real, than another, but to suggest that constructionism provides for the possibility of differing constructions of the same experience, whilst positivism suggests there is just one objective truth of that experience.

Snape and Spencer (2003) highlight the key assumptions of this approach as:

- The researcher and the social world impact on each other.
- Facts and values are not distinct and findings are inevitably influenced by the researcher's perspective and values, thus making it impossible to conduct objective value free research, although the researcher can declare and be transparent about his or her assumptions.
- The methods of the natural sciences are not appropriate because the social world is not governed by law-like regularities but is mediated through meaning and human agency; consequently the social researcher is concerned to explore and

understand the social world using both the participant's and the researcher's understanding. (Snape and Spencer, 2003: 17)

❖ Pragmatic knowledge claims

Following on from concerns about the constructivist and positivist approaches and their alignments to quantitative and qualitative techniques respectively has been the development of pragmatism. Pragmatism has its roots within the works of Mead and Dewey. There are a number of forms of pragmatism but most share a common belief that knowledge arises out of actions, situations and consequences and a concern with applications and 'what works' (Patton, 1990). For the pragmatist it isn't the methods that are important – it is the problem; and researchers need to use whatever research methods that are required to address the problem. Pragmatism opens the door to mixed method approaches that in other circumstances would be frowned upon. Creswell (2007) sums up the key features of pragmatism:

- Pragmatism is not committed to any one system of philosophy and reality.
- Individual members have a freedom of choice – to choose the methods, techniques, and procedures of research that best meet their needs and purposes.
- Pragmatists do not see the world as an absolute unity.
- Truth is what works at the time; it is not based in a strict dualism between the mind and a reality completely independent of the mind.
- Pragmatist researchers look to 'what' and 'how' to research based on its intended consequences – where they want to go with it. Mixed methods researchers need to establish a purpose for their 'mixing', a rationale for the reasons why quantitative and qualitative data need to be mixed in the first place.
- Pragmatists agree that research always occurs in social, hierarchical, political and other contexts.
- Pragmatists believe that we need to stop asking questions about reality and the laws of nature. (Creswell, 2007: 12)

In particular the pragmatic approach emphasizes the position that no one research method is automatically better than any other. The pragmatist argues that what matters is using the best research method or methods to answer the research question as fully as possible. We will return to some of the claims of the pragmatists and mixed methods as part of our discussions about methodology.

❖ *Advocacy/participatory knowledge claims*

Both positivism and social constructionism have been criticized for their conservative stances and acceptance of the status quo. Positivist assumptions impose structural laws and theories that do not fit with marginalized individuals' or groups' experience or address issues of social justice, whereas constructivist stances do not go far enough in advocating an agenda to support marginalized peoples (Cresswell, 2003). In response to this criticism an alternative approach has been developed whose body of work has been influenced by Marx, Adorno, Marcuse, Habermas and Friere (Neuman, 2000) whose work was all intertwined with politics and a political agenda. The advocacy/participatory approach would emphasize those constructions of reality become manifest not through the 'mind' but, through reflective action. As Reason (1998: 279) states: 'knowledge arises in and for action'. In particular, this action should contain an agenda for reform that addresses issues to promote empowerment, reduce inequality and address issues of oppression for participants, the organizations or groups in which they work. The advocacy/participatory approach adheres to a social model perspective, emphasizing that it is society that disables individuals, not their health conditions or memberships of disenfranchised or marginalized groups.

Accountability for research in such circumstances is to the members of such groups and their organizations and a commitment to producing empowering research both in terms of process and in terms of outcomes (Barnes, 2004). At the heart of this approach is an acceptance that the researcher is not an objective neutral participant in the process. Research is seen not just as an end in itself but a process which has victimized marginalized group members in the past, and advocacy/participatory research provides an opportunity to reverse this trend into an empowering process. For this approach the generation of new knowledge is an inadequate justification for research. Research is only justified when it is accompanied by change (Glasby and Beresford, 2006).

Within these knowledge claims are a number of disparate groups whom society may have marginalized or disenfranchised and whose identification helps construct an agenda for the issues to be researched. These approaches may include feminist perspectives, racialized discourses, critical theory, queer theory or disability inquiry. This is not an exhaustive list and the reader will also be aware that it is possible to be a member of more than one group.

Creswell (2007) identifies the key features of advocacy or participatory forms of inquiry as:

- Participatory action is recursive or dialectical and is focussed on bringing about change in practice.

- It is focussed on helping individuals free themselves from constraints found in the media, in language, in work procedures and in relationships of power in educational settings.
- It is emancipatory in that it helps unshackle people from the constraints of irrational and unjust structures that limit self-development and self-determination.
- It is practical and collaborative because it is inquiry completed 'with' others rather than 'on' or 'to' others. In this spirit advocacy/ participatory authors engage the participants as active collaborators in their inquiries. (Creswell, 2007: 11)

From the above it is clear that this approach is one that would be inherently attractive to many of those who support the involvement of service users in research and for service users who wish to become involved in research to promote changes. This perspective and its links with service user co-researchers will be discussed in greater detail later in this chapter.

Methodology

Methodology is not the same as method. Research methods are the concrete techniques or technical practices used to identify research questions, gather and analyse data.

> At their simplest, they are a tool, in the same way we use a hammer to drive in nails. Provided we hit the nails without bending them, there should be no problems – although we do need to be sure the nail is the right fixing, the right size, and that the wood won't split. Note, we do not use a hammer to drive in a screw, or a screwdriver to put in a nail. In other words, our simple view of the tool actually hides the fact that, at a second level, its use is governed by limitations: it has to be used correctly, and it has to be the correct tool for the job. (Payne and Payne, 2004: 149)

Methodology, on the other hand, refers to the ways in which we acquire knowledge. Whereas ontology is concerned with 'the study of being', epistemology with 'what is knowledge', methodology refers to the ways in which knowledge is acquired, and the basic question for methodology is 'How do we know?' (Moses and Knutsen, 2007). As such, methods are important to methodology, but it is the methodology which should decide upon the methods, not the other way around. For once a methodology is adopted the choice of method(s) becomes a technical, not a philosophical decision.

Different methodologies provide different lenses to view the same situation. Moses and Knutzen (2007) usefully use the analogy of the practice of 'medical professionals' and 'homeopathic practitioners' to highlight the importance of methodology. It is clear that both of these professional groups provide competing ways of understanding and promoting human well-being. Methodology provides the different medical bags used by the different practitioners and we would expect a minor crisis if the bags of the medical and homeopathic healers where to be switched. Of course, there may be some instruments that are common to both bags, but how these are used in practice will vary. The toolbox analogy may be quite simple, but it does highlight the difference between methods and methodology.

In a literal sense methodology refers to the science or study of methods, and as such it seeks to explore the characteristics and principles on which methods are based and the standards governing their selection and application (Payne and Payne, 2004). Unfortunately, methodology is used in at least two other ways. Researchers often refer to the 'methodology used in this study', using methodology as a synonym for methods as it sounds grander and more scientific. Also for others, by referring to methods as 'methodology' they are referring to the conceptual baggage associated with the term. In doing so the use of the term 'methodology' refers to the grander philosophical understandings which underpin the researcher's work. 'Methodology' in this sense is often used as a justificatory technique legitimizing choice of research subject, methods and findings. If someone says they have adopted a feminist or interprevist methodology we are provided with an insight into the sets of values the researcher brought to their study. At best this helps us to understand their assumptions about the world, how it may be known and helps us to assess their findings. At worst it masks questions about topic selection, making these appear self-evident. If methods are supposed to follow the research question, who and what determines the research question in the first place? Unsurprisingly researchers find it more comfortable to use conceptual frameworks, study topics and use methods which align to their own personal orientation. This is not to say that those who prefer to use qualitative approaches will not also use quantitative approaches, but that they will feel more at ease with their own bias.

Generally researchers talk of two traditions in methods: quantitative and qualitative. The next two sections will explore the basic assumption of each approach. These two methodological traditions should be viewed as ideal types. Ideal types do not exist independently in the world but provide a conceptual differentiation which makes the world easier to comprehend. An ideal type is a simplified model of a complicated world, highlighting differences and minimizing similarities creating an artificial dualism.

❖ *Quantitative methods*

Quantitative and qualitative are shorthand ways of referring to the two major approaches to research methods. 'Quantitative methods' is an umbrella term covering a wide range of different types of research (Bryman, 1988).

> Quantitative methods (normally using deductive logic) seek regularities in human lives, by separating the social world into empirical components called variables which can be represented numerically as frequencies or rate, whose associations with each other can be explored by statistical techniques, and accessed through researcher-introduced stimuli and systematic measurement. (Payne and Payne, 2004: 180)

Payne and Payne go on to identify five common features shared by most quantitative techniques:

- The core concern is to describe and *account for regularities in social behaviour.*
- Patterns of behaviour can be *separated out into variable, and represented by numbers.*
- Explanations are expressed as *associations* (usually statistical) *between variables.*
- They explore social phenomena not just as they naturally occur, but by introducing *stimuli* like survey questions, collecting data by *systematic, repeated and controlled measurements.*
- They are based on the assumption that *social processes exist outside of individual actors' comprehension,* constraining individual actions, and accessible to researchers by virtue of their prior theoretical and empirical knowledge. (Payne and Payne, 2004: 181–2, italics in original)

Strategies associated with quantitative methods include experiments, quasi experiments (that use non-randomized designs or single subject designs) and surveys. The 'gold standard' of quantitative approaches for assessing the efficacy of treatment methods is random control trials (RCT) (Reynolds, 2000). RCTs, as the name suggests, require a random allocation of potential participants into an experimental and control group. The experimental group may then be further split in half between a group receiving the treatment and a group who receive a placebo. The intention of this randomized splitting is to eliminate bias, ensuring neither research participants nor those treating the participants are aware of who has been allocated to which experimental group. Similarly, those evaluating the outcomes should be unaware of who has received which treatment. The results are then evaluated to identify the relative outcomes and whether there is a statistically significant relationship between outcomes and treatment methods in comparison with the control group. There are, however, potential difficulties with RCTs, depending on whose perspective is given greatest significance. For example, the clinical significance may be interpreted differently by an anaesthetist (the patient survived the operation); the surgeon (the patient was discharged from hospital); the district nurse (the patient was still alive/survived six months after the operation); the carer (their loved one is now more independent); and the research participant or service user, who is now able to walk to the shops.

❖ Qualitative methods

Qualitative methods are linked to the constructionist or interpretist philosophical perspectives. Their focus is to interpret and construct how ordinary people observe and describe their lives in natural settings. In so doing qualitative methods generally produce detailed non-quantitative accounts and use induction to help interpret the meanings people make of their lives. Payne and Payne (2004) have summed up the key features of qualitative methods as:

- Focus on seeking out and interpreting the meanings that people ascribe to their actions.
- Actions are seen as contextualised, holistic and part of a social process.
- Seek to encounter social phenomena as they naturally occur.
- They work with smaller samples looking for depth and detail of meaning with a less general and abstracted level of explanation.
- They use inductive as opposed to deductive logic, allowing ideas to emerge as they explore the data. (Payne and Payne, 2004: 175–6)

Qualitative approaches have thus developed their own methods including participant observation and focus groups, although techniques like grounded theory (Strauss and Corbin, 1987), ethnography (Hammersley, 1998) and narrative research (Clandinin and Connolly, 2000), are not only methods, but also methodologies in their own right.

❖ Mixed methods

There are at least three ways of understanding mixed methods. The first accepts that there are research methods, like questionnaires and interviews, that can be either quantitative, using closed questions and rating scales, or qualitative, using open questions. It is also not unusual to have both types of questions in the same interview or questionnaire schedule. The closed questions may be attempting to gain a comparative view of a particular practice, for example, how people with learning disabilities are treated by GPs. The statistical perspective may provide details of the percentage of people with learning disabilities who are seen by GPs in terms of the frequencies of visits, age distributions, non-attendances at surgeries, types of illnesses and a satisfaction scale for the service. What closed questions will not be able to tell you is how these judgements have been arrived at, what the experience of visiting a GP is like or how barriers could be reduced or practices developed to promote greater access to GP services. Without the open questions we will not know what the outcomes from the closed questions are outcomes of.

The second meaning of mixed methods is when a number of methods are used from the same methodology within the research. This may take the shape of using focus groups to establish the issues that are most important for cancer sufferers and then using open ended questions in an interview format to look at these issues in much greater depth. The focus group allows you to highlight the key areas through a group process which can then be explored and checked out in a one-to-one situation.

The third meaning of mixed methods comes from the pragmatist's view of research methodology where 'what works' is what matters, and it is the research question that should drive which research methods should be used. There is some debate about whether this leads to a lack of 'analytical clarity' (Snape and Spencer, 2003) because each method is informed by a different and mutually excluding assumption on how knowledge claims make the reconciliation of different data techniques impossible:

> Every research tool or procedure is extricably embedded in commitments to particular versions of the world and to knowing the world. To use a questionnaire, to use an attitude scale, to take the role of a participant observer, to select a random sample, to measure rates of population, and so on, is to be involved in conceptions of the world which allow these instruments to be used for the purposes conceived. No technique or method of investigation (and this is as true of the natural sciences as it is of the social) is self-validating: its effectiveness, i.e. its very status as a research instrument making the world tractable to investigation, is, from a philosophical point of view, ultimately dependent on epistemological justifications. (Hughes, 1990: 11)

From Hughes's perspective all research methods are imbued with their own philosophical baggage and that researchers need to be careful not to use contradictory philosophical knowledge claims as this would both contaminate and undermine the research. Ritchie, writing in a book on qualitative research practice, takes a more measured view of how different methods can be integrated by acknowledging that:

> When using qualitative and quantitative research in harness, it is important to recognise each offers a different way of knowing about the world. Although they may well be addressing the same research issue, they will provide a different 'reading' or form of calibration on that issue. As a consequence, it should not be expected that the evidence generated from the two approaches will replicate each other. Instead the purpose of interlocking qualitative and quantitative data is to achieve an extended understanding that neither method alone can offer. It is then up to the researcher to explain why the data and their 'meaning' are different. (Ritchie, 2003: 43)

This view acknowledges that qualitative and quantitative methods can be combined in the same study where to do so would be helpful in answering the research question and demonstrating additionality over the use of just qualitative or quantitative approaches. This view also highlights that we should not expect that qualitative and quantitative methodologies will provide the same answers but should expect differences which will challenge the researcher for explanation.

Cresswell (2003) identifies three major strategies for mixed methods: sequential, concurrent and transformative procedures. Sequential procedures are when the researcher elaborates the findings of one method by the use of another method. Concurrent procedures occur when the researcher converges quantitative and qualitative approaches in order to develop a more detailed analysis of the research problem. Transformative procedures occur when the researcher uses an overarching theoretical perspective or lens, e.g. feminism, within a study that contains both quantitative and qualitative methods.

How qualitative and quantitative approaches are reconciled is not necessarily straightforward. Researchers are unlikely to give up on their preferences. For example, at a recent ESRC research training event on mixed methods, a well-known medical sociologist commented upon how credibility within her field researchers have had to be quantitative in orientation but are now adding some qualitative methods to their research proposals, which in essence still remain driven from a quantitative perspective. D'Cruz and Jones (2004), approaching the same issue from the opposite end of the spectrum, talk of how they use quantitative research as an addition to their preferred qualitative research in social work to ensure policy makers will treat their research seriously. Neither position could properly be described as truly mixed methods as both are potential examples of a 'tick box' mentality, where the reluctant inclusion of an alternative research method is to hoodwink an influential audience.

Service user knowledge claims

In this section we begin to unpick the knowledge claims of including service users in research. In particular we look at this in terms of 'traditional' research, service user standpoint research and the possibility of an alternative research methodology and method.

Reflexive Questions

✳ Back at the start of this chapter you were asked to consider whether you thought there was a difference between the knowledge claims of research involving service users as researchers and research that did not include service users. Given what you have read in this chapter so far, has your position changed? If not, why not? If so why?

Traditional knowledge claims and involving service users in research

It is quite clear that involving service users in research is justified in terms of making traditional knowledge claims. Reading the published literature suggests that service users are less likely to be involved in research that flows from realism with its ontological perspective than there is an external world that exists independently of the knower. This should not be surprising, as service users who become involved in research, like many other researchers, have an attachment to the issues they wish to explore. It thus makes sense that service users would prefer to be involved in those issues that accept that who and what we are affects how we make sense of, or understand the world. Thus a subtle realism or idealism position is likely to be more acceptable to service users. This is not to suggest that service users cannot usefully contribute to traditional quantitative research; this is patently not the case. For example, they may be involved in a steering or reference group for the research or may input into the questions asked. They may also be involved with the distribution of the questionnaires due to their insider knowledge of where service users congregate. This may be particularly helpful where you are dealing with groups of harder to reach service users – for example, people who misuse drugs, or younger gay men. However, besides these areas the service user co-researchers are primarily acting as traditional research assistants. This will also be the case if they are involved with the analysis which is likely to be statistically oriented and will rely less on the service user's experience and more on their mathematical ability. Barnes and Mercer (2006) note that in disability research quantitative methods are often seen as inherently exploitive of research participants, emphasizing the division between the research 'expert' and lay disabled respondent.

In this section we are suggesting that although service users can be and are involved in quantitative research projects their involvement is likely to be more limited than it can be in qualitative research. As Humphries (2003) notes, participatory research is often associated with qualitative research, but this does not necessarily have to be the case. Nevertheless it is not surprising that involving service users in qualitative research is likely to play to service users' concerns about 'having a voice' and 'authenticity'. These methods have an emphasis upon meaning and understanding and are likely to employ methods requiring the interpretation and the social construction of experience where service users' own experiences are likely to come to the fore. In qualitative research service user co-researchers can potentially be involved in all aspects of the research process. Although, again service user involvement in the more advanced qualitative techniques will be dependent upon their skill levels.

It is clear from the above that service user co-researchers can make a significant contribution to knowledge claims within both quantitative and qualitative frameworks. It will thus be evident that they will also have a significant contribution to make to mixed method approaches. Involving service users as co-researchers will be explored through the research cycle in much greater detail in the next two chapters, but before moving on we need to explore the developing thrust that the only knowledge claims worth making derive from service users, or a 'standpoint position' of knowledge claims for involving service users as co-researchers.

❖ Service user research and standpoint epistemology

Standpoint theory is where knowledge claims are dependent on someone's membership of a particular social group. For example, feminist standpoint theory ascribed privileged insight to women, or in particular to feminists engaged in the struggle for women's emancipation (Harding, 1986). Researchers like Stanley and Wise (1983) placed an emphasis on the capacity of female researchers to understand other women, to the point that it was being suggested that only a woman could interview another woman. In relation to service user research we can see certain similarities where there has been an emancipatory struggle and on occasions the rallying cry of 'no research about us without us' raises the question as to what are the grounds for accepting that one group has a superior insight into reality than another. It cannot be just because they say so. Beresford (2000: 493) makes the claim in relation to social care, but this claim could just as easily be applied to health settings:

> One key quality distinguishes such (service user) knowledges from all others involved in social care and social policy provision. They alone are based on *direct* experience of such policy and provision from the *receiving end*, service users' knowledges grow out of their personal and collective experience of policy, practice and services. They also explicitly emphasize this. They are not based solely on an intellectual, occupational or political concern. As in all identity based groupings and movements they are experientially based.

In this article Beresford is staking a claim for a privileged position for service users who are on the receiving end of services and policies. By being recipients, service users experience the effects of policies, both intended and unintended, and are therefore in a better position than service providers or academics to know what is required to change a situation. Service users are able to see the policies and services both from the perspective of being a recipient of the policies and services but also from the point of view of what is required to make a difference in their lives. From this perspective service users are best placed to generate critical questions and knowledge claims. Whilst Beresford is right to challenge academic knowledge and the oppressive way in which academic research has sought to categorize service users, it is another thing to replace oppression by academics with oppression by service users. Hammersley (1995: 71) makes the point:

> While we must recognise that people in different social locations may have divergent perspectives giving them distinctive insights, it is not clear why we should believe the implausible claim that some category of people has privileged access to knowledge whilst others are blinded by ideology.

Nolan et al. (2007a) go further than this and contend that privileging user-controlled research is itself potentially a form of oppression, as it assumes all service users want to exercise this level of control when the evidence does not support this viewpoint (Turner and Beresford, 2005a; Dewar, 2005). Barnes and Mercer (2006) also comment, in relation to disability research, that whilst some researchers would claim the need to choose a disabled person as an interviewer of other disabled people it is not clear how far they would take the matching process. Does it also need to cover, age, gender, ethnicity, sexuality, social class, religion or type of impairment? Having an impairment, or being a service user, does not automatically provide someone with an affinity for other service users, nor does it necessarily make someone a good researcher.

If we accept Barnes and Hammersley's assertion, it is then important to identify some rationale against which knowledge claims can be assessed. If we accept that service users as co-researchers have an important contribution to make to knowledge creation we then need to be able to assess the validity of the knowledge claims. This is an imperative if you agree that research that fails to include the knowledge service users have of themselves in relation to a policy, practice, service or medical intervention is missing an important piece of the jigsaw. This is a far cry from claiming that everyone else's research on the same subject is necessarily invalid if it does not include the service user's voice. To be able to say that either position is invalid we need to go beyond standpoint theory and consider the following norms:

- The overriding concern of the researcher is the truth of claims, not their political implications or practical consequences.
- Arguments are not judged on the basis of the personal and/or social characteristics of the person advancing them, but solely in terms of their plausibility and credibility.
- Researchers are willing to change their views if arguments from common ground suggest that those views are false; and equally important, they assume (and behave as if) fellow researchers have the same attitude – at least until there is very strong evidence otherwise.
- Where agreement does not result, all parties must recognize that there remains some reasonable doubt about the validity of their own positions, so that whenever the latter are presented they require supporting arguments, or reference to where such argument can be found.
- The research community is open to participation by anyone able and willing to operate on the basis of the first four rules; though their contributions will be judged wanting if they lack sufficient knowledge of the field and/or of relevant methodology. In particular, there must be no restrictions of participation on the grounds of religious or political attitudes. (Hammersley, 1995: 76)

To Hammersley's last point it is possible to add there should be no restriction of access to the research community by those who are service users or those who are not. The criterion for a research identity thus becomes dependent on research skills, not on one's identity as a service user or not. This is not to claim that researchers should be totally ignorant of the subjects they study and there are occasions when it is possible to be 'too distant' from the experiences being interpreted. A famous example of this would have been Miller and Gwynne's (1972) study of institutionalized disabled people which rejected the experiential knowledge of the disabled research participants. However, this is not to advocate for research as a form of propaganda. There are many ways in which research is inherently political but needs to avoid merely serving political purposes or positions and instead challenge accepted positions through the development of new knowledge from researchers and service users alike which can then be utilized to support change.

Pawson et al. (2003) analysed the way in which knowledge could be categorized in social care and concluded it could best be identified by its source. They identified five key sources:

- Organisational knowledge – to do with governance and policies.
- Practitioner knowledge – personal, context specific often tacit.
- User knowledge – first hand experience and reflection, often unspoken and undervalued.
- Research knowledge – the most 'plausible' source but requiring a 'broad church' interpretation of research
- Policy community – concerning societal and political drivers determining the issues of significance. (Pawson et al., 2003 quoted in Nolan et al., 2007a: 9)

They argued that none of the different ways was necessarily better than any of the others; but that neither should we assume that all the sources are of equal merit on all occasions.

Conclusion

Back at the start of this chapter you were asked to consider whether you thought there was a difference between the knowledge claims of research involving service users as researchers and research that did not include service users. The argument in this chapter leans towards an answer of both yes and no. No, service users as researchers have access to all the same research tools and perspectives as any other researcher. Their ability to develop knowledge claims will depend on their expertise with the tools. Yes, there is a difference in that their very position as service users gives them a different experiential perspective which potentially provides an extra element to understanding a situation more fully than a traditional researcher who has not had that experience. This benefit though can become a liability if the service user co-researcher becomes so blinded by their own experience that they are unable to see any other perspective or viewpoint.

Service user involvement as researchers in the development of knowledge claims is possible in the different ontologies and epistemologies we have described. However, how this is translated into practice is very different. Within a realist quantitative approach the service user contribution is likely to be very limited given its notion about research objectivity, distance and the nature of knowledge generation. At best the service user co-researcher can be viewed as a research assistant whose experiences of using a service are not valued for the knowledge and insights they provide. Within more qualitative, social constructionist approaches it is this experiential knowledge that is valued and in which the development of research skills can be used to improve the research quality. We also looked at mixed method approaches which seek to eschew theory and work from a pragmatist point of view, involving both types of approaches and focusing on how best to answer the research question. We have also reviewed the standpoint theory as an offshoot of social constructionism and incorporating a political dimension and commitment to change. It is easy to see why this approach is particularly valued by service user co-researchers and resonates with their experiences of services. However, we also identified some of the dangers of this approach and its claims to knowledge and dangers of becoming merely propaganda and thereby undermining service user co-researcher contributions to research. From this review of knowledge claims it should be clear to the reader that although there are a number of different ways of understanding these questions from the ontological, epistemological and methodological perspectives, no one approach will satisfy all circumstances or is likely to be relevant in all cases. For example, if we are seeking to establish the effectiveness of a new drug, randomized control trials may be the most suitable method, but it will not be if we are seeking to understand the experience of being admitted to a hospital ward or to an elderly person's home. In this chapter we have sought to establish a space for knowledge claims from service users' involvement in research. This place is contested and contestable, but adds to a richer understanding of health and social care knowledge claims. Such claims are not privileged but need to be seen in light of the research question and the ontological, epistemological and methodological responses to the research question, accepting both the strengths and weakness of different approaches. There is clearly a place for service user researchers and co-researchers in health and social care research. However, this place needs to be supported by credible and valid research – but, what credible and valid are – are open to debate and justification.

Summary

In this chapter we have undertaken a short exploration of the philosophy of research. In particular we highlighted ontology – the study of being, epistemology – what is knowledge and methodology – how do we know? Within each term we explored a range of different ways of answering each question and also looked at a range of methods, including quantitative, qualitative and mixed method approaches. We were able to demonstrate that although it is possible to argue for service user involvement in all the different ways of developing knowledge claims there are some which promised a more active involvement and will resonate more closely with service user aspirations than others. However, there is no philosophical reason why service users should be refused access to knowledge creation although there will be limits to what they can do (as there would be for any professional researcher). These limits will be partly to do with the vision of research commissioners, the levels of research skills and the nature of the problem to be researched. Like any other researcher, service user researchers will be able to develop more or less accurate knowledge claims.

Recommended reading

There is currently no textbook that deals substantively with the philosophical and knowledge claims made for service users as co-researchers. The following texts have thus to be read with the challenges of the service user perspective in mind.

Barnes, C. and Mercer, G. (1997) (eds) *Doing Disability Research*. Leeds: The Disability Press. Also available at www.leeds.ac.uk/disability-studies/archiveuk/index.html. This provides a good example of the justification and practice of advocacy/participatory research.

Beresford, P. (2000) 'Service users' knowledge and social work theory: conflict or collaboration?, *British Journal of Social Work*, 30 (4): 489–504.

Creswell, J. W. (2003) Research *Design: Qualitative, Quantitative and Mixed Methods Approaches*. London: Sage. A useful justification for mixed method approaches and in particular how they can be used together to create additionality.

Crotty, M. (2003) *The Foundation of Social Research: Meaning and Perspective in the Research Process*. London: Sage. A more challenging book on the philosophical perspectives and issues.

Hammersley, M. (1995) *The Politics of Social Research*. London: Sage. Although older it is a very well written, stimulating and challenging book.

Nolan, M., Hanson, E., Grant, G., Keady, J. and Magnusson, L. (2007) 'Introduction: what counts as knowledge, whose knowledge counts? Towards authentic participatory enquiry', in M. Nolan, E. Hanson, G. Grant, and J. Keady (eds). *User Participation in Health and Social Care Research*. Maidenhead: Open University Press, pp. 1–13. An accessible introduction to many of the key issues.

Ritchie, J. and Lewis, J. (2003) (eds) *Qualitative Research Practice: A Guide for Social Sciences Students and Researchers*. London: Sage. A good guide to qualitative methods generally; however the first two chapters are particularly relevant to this chapter.

5 Practical Issues and Stumbling Blocks: From Conception to Data Collection

Introduction

In this, and the next chapter, we focus on 'how' to meaningfully involve service users as co-researchers in the research process. This is a major part of the book and has been split into two chapters. This chapter will follow the research process from the point of the research's conception to the point of data collection. The next chapter will then follow this through to the point of research dissemination. In particular this chapter will highlight the practical issues surrounding research conception, peer review of research proposals, service user co-researcher recruitment, training of co-researchers, literature review, the establishment of reference and steering groups, barriers to involvement and the development of research tools. There is an obvious link between these two chapters and Chapter 3 on ethics. Issues like reward and recognition cover both ethical and practical issues and could have been covered in either chapter. The current split between ethics and practical issues is to allow us to highlight individual issues, and the reader needs to be aware that because they have been located in one or other chapter is not to suggest that they do not have ethical or practical implications.

Research conception

The idea to undertake research with service user co-researchers has to come from somewhere. In Chapter 3 we looked at the issue of who funds research and in particular the ethical challenge of obtaining acceptable funding and avoiding being used as a means by which certain companies can launder their image. This chapter examines this issue from a different perspective. The notion of involving service users as co-researchers can come from a number of different sources. The idea may have resulted from the service users themselves who wish to commission research to look at services or concerns that are close to their heart. This can be to provide support for change in current service provision so that it is more in line with their needs. Conversely, the opposite may be true as the research may be to provide evidence that the same services should be retained or developed further rather than changed or closed down. The second of these reasons may be a reaction to a health authority's or local authority's desire to withdraw or re-design a service. In these instances the service users are wishing to use research to help 'improve' or retain the services they receive. The famous Le Court home request to Miller and Gwynne (1972) did not involve a request to be involved as researchers but was a commission of researchers to examine their 'living' situation. Similarly it is quite possible for other groups to request research although there is likely to be a major challenge in terms of obtaining external funding by service user groups, which in itself is likely to require some help from professional researchers.

There are also a number of researchers who are also service users. There are those, like Professors Colin Barnes and Peter Beresford, who define themselves both as researchers and as service users. Each can lay claim to expertise in both conducting research and of having experience (or continuing to experience) what it means to be a service user. There are others, like Wilson (Wilson and Beresford, 2000) who do not wish to be identified and so use a pseudonym. Wilson states she, if it is a she, is a psychiatric system survivor and part-time social work tutor. It can only be surmised that she feels her identity as a psychiatric survivor would somehow create personal or professional problems if this became known or that her psychiatric survivor status would undermine the arguments in the article. For whatever reason, Anne Wilson is a pseudonym and it can only be surmised that her negative identity as a psychiatric survivor precludes her identifying who she really is.

Researchers like Barnes and Beresford also raise a particular conundrum for service user research, as both are advocates within the service user movement and both are eminent researchers heading up academic research centres – the Centre for Disability Studies and Centre for Citizen Participation, respectively. Hodgson and Canvin (2005: 55) writing about health research ask:

> What depth of knowledge do consumers need to be participants in health research? Do consumers have the same or equivalent knowledge as researchers? If consumers do not have the requisite technical expertise, must they be trained? And, if they receive such training, do they then become researchers and cease to be consumers? If consumers' lay expertise and (research) naivety are at the core of why their involvement might be valuable to health research, their integration into the social world of research seems to contradict, indeed disable this contribution as their conformity to the dominant discourse of health research pervades the way in which we see the world.

It is interesting to question how Barnes and Beresford would answer this challenge as to whether they are to be seen primarily as researchers or as service users. Their experience of using services has obviously impacted upon their choice of research subject. It also remains an open question whether their research training has, or has not, impacted upon the ways in which they experience the world and whether this is a help or hindrance to researching service user experiences. This is not to claim that service users cannot become eminent researchers; the idea is obviously preposterous. However, there is a question as to whether in doing so they become socialized into the research world and as such lose some of the cutting edge of their experiential world which becomes mediated through academic understandings. It could also be claimed that their academic training has helped them to more fully understand their service user experience. Whichever position you may wish to take, research and service user organizations would be poorer without role models like Barnes and Beresford, who are not only part of the academic world but supporters of service user involvement in research. This conundrum will be re-visited in the next chapter in relation to those service users who become involved as researchers in one research project and then wish to continue to develop as researchers whilst retaining their service user identity.

We have so far discussed the difficulties of service users commissioning and funding their own research. An alternative way that service users as co-researchers has been developing is through the commitment of a growing number of researchers who see this as an important way of researching issues in health and social care. The issues covered include cancer care (Stevens et al., 2005), children who use NHS services (Moules, 2005), user led disability services (Barnes and Mercer, 2006), learning disabilities (Williams and England, 2005; McClimens, 2007), mental health (Clark et al., 2005; Waldham, 2005) or child protection (McLaughlin, 2005). There is thus a growing critical mass of researchers who see service users as co-researchers as an effective and credible method for the development of health and social care research. If service users' organizations are unable to identify funding for potential research projects researchers may be able to do so. If researchers have identified funding it is important that they involve potential co-researchers in the research plan as soon as possible. This can be difficult as some research commissioners will want to be clear from the outset how resources are to be used and the nature of service user co-researcher involvement in the research. The longer service user co-researchers are kept out of the decision-making processes concerning a research project the less collaborative the project is likely to be. This is not to say that it is not possible to act in a collaborative way in other parts of the research process but this is more difficult if the commissioners reduce the room for manoeuvre and the opportunity to influence. Ideally the service user co-researchers should be recruited before the research bid has been completed. However, as stated previously, this can have difficulties for research commissioners and ethics committees, who would frown upon researchers working with service users before ethical approval has been secured. Also, co-researchers are unlikely to be paid for participating in a bid that has not yet been approved, whilst it should also be remembered that most research bids are unsuccessful. In an innovative project in Trent it is possible to obtain grants of up to £500 to involve service users in pre-protocol work.

Before we move on to the recruitment of potential service user co-researchers, it is worth considering other opportunities for service users to be involved in research and in particular acting as peer reviewers or members of research commissioning boards.

Peer review of research proposals

It is standard practice for research proposals to be reviewed by peers. Peer reviewing is part of the research commissioning process where a research proposal is read and commented upon to help inform commissioners which research grant applications to support (INVOLVE, 2006a). Peer reviewing usually involves commenting on whether the research addresses an important and relevant question and whether the methods by which the researcher seeks to address the question will provide the answers they require. This latter point may include the nature of service user involvement in the research proposal. Organizations like the government funded SCIE and the National Health Institute for Health Research have regularly asked service users to act as peer reviewers. In particular, service users can provide experiential perspectives on the questions being asked, ensuring that they are pertinent and important to those who experience the service, or condition, and that the proposed method of involving service users is relevant. Service users need no prior formal qualifications to be a peer reviewer but would need to have an experiential understanding of the subject under scrutiny and a willingness to familiarize themselves with the specialist research and health and social care language (INVOLVE, 2006a).

The peer reviewing of research proposals offers another opportunity, although not well publicized, for members of the public and those who use health and social care services to influence which research proposals are funded. Once a peer review report is completed it is sent to the research commissioners for the research commissioning board to consider.

Service user members of research commissioning boards

A commissioning board is a group of people who oversee the **commissioning** process. It is made up of research funders, researchers, health and/or social care professionals and often includes people who use services and carers. The key role of a commissioning board is to assess **research grant applications** that have been submitted and ensure that those selected for funding are relevant and of high quality. (INVOLVE, 2006b: 1; bold in original)

Commissioning boards usually have terms of reference and are made up of a range of specialists which may include a service user. The purpose of commissioning boards is to consider which research proposals should be funded and which should not. This will include looking at the peer reviewer's comments. The commissioning board is likely to meet as a group, but may also be conducted as a virtual group via email or as an electronic discussion board. Service users are valued members on such groups for their experience of the condition or service under review, their ability to identify priority areas for research and to advise on the strategy to involve service users or identify research respondents. It is not to be assumed that all the members of the commissioning board will agree on who to fund and who not to fund. The board will have a process for making decisions which may be based on a simple majority basis. It is common practice for boards to contain more than one service user member. It is likely that service users will have to complete an application form to become a member of a commissioning body and it would be helpful if they could demonstrate experience of being a member of other committees, have good communication skills and a willingness to familiarize themselves with specialist research and health and social care language. As can be seen, there are obvious overlaps between the peer reviewing and the work of research commissioning boards, both of which offer opportunities for service users to become more involved in influencing which research is conducted and to help contribute to the improvement of research that is approved.

Recruitment of potential service users as co-researchers

Reflexive Questions

✳ Can you think of a research proposal or service evaluation that you would like to undertake? Now consider whether your research would benefit from involving service user co-researchers. You may want to write the idea down and follow the same proposal through the next set of reflective questions. Having decided upon a research proposal, can you now identify where and how you would identify the service users to act as co-researchers?

At some point early in the research process service user co-researchers will need to be recruited. In order to do this the lead researcher needs to be aware of both the number of co-researchers required and the types of activities they are required to do. It may be possible to work with an already established group of service users, place an advert in places attended by the target group or to use a snowball effect. The snowball effect of recruiting is where one member of a service user group is recruited and they are then asked to identify another service user who can be recruited and so on until sufficient numbers of service users have been recruited. Such techniques are particularly useful for more sensitive, stigmatized or hard to reach groups, like single parents who use illegal drugs, or young people with sexually transmitted diseases, which may take time and a lot of effort. Whatever method is used it will to some extent depend on what groups or organizations are available and the nature of the research. It should not be assumed that because there is a group already in existence that this group will necessarily be inclusive and contain all those who may wish to become co-researchers or to act as research respondents. McLaughlin et al. (2004) describe a situation where a local authority wanted to consult with D/deaf service users about current service provision and sought to use the local D/deaf club. On the surface this appears to be a reasonable suggestion until it was identified that the centre was not used by young black people within the borough. Thus any conclusions that could have been drawn from those who attended the day centre would be at best partial and at worst misleading and could not be considered as reflective of the D/deaf community.

In seeking to recruit co-researchers personal contact is most important as potential co-researchers need to feel they are able to work with an academic researcher just as much as the lead researcher should feel confident about working with them. It is important that in recruiting potential research respondents not to silence potential voices or to further disempower excluded groups. Issues such as age, ethnicity, gender, disability, sexual orientation and social class need to be considered alongside issues like travelling distances, an urban–rural split or even which types of food are offered. This process should be as transparent and inclusive as possible to addressing possible allegations of favouritism, racism, homophobia, 'cherry picking' and so on. From the beginning it is important to ensure that a participatory research process should be seen as inclusive and avoid denying participation on irrelevant grounds or through lack of planning and consideration.

In recruiting service user co-researchers there is often a belief that any such recruitment should be representative or that any service users recruited are typical of service users using that service. It is obviously quite difficult for a few people to represent all service users using a particular service just as it is unlikely to assume that one or two service providers could be representative of all service providers.

It is highly unlikely that there is only 'one' service user voice. You only need to remember our earlier discussion of Turner and Beresford's (2005a) finding that service users were, understandably, unable to agree whether service user controlled research meant that professional researchers could be used or not used in the research process. Service users are not a homogeneous group and the Association of Directors of Social Services usefully drew up guidelines for the involvement of service users, indicating that service users and carers contribute to service development through their experiences, not their representativeness (Jones, 1995). This is also highlighted by Hanley et al. (2004: 5):

> In essence it is not reasonable to expect one or two people to be representative of all people who use similar services. But then it is not reasonable to expect one doctor to be representative of all doctors either. It might be helpful to reframe this in terms of thinking about seeking **perspectives** rather than representativeness; if you want a range of perspectives, involve a range of people. (bold in original)

If we are seeking a representative sample of service users to act as co-researchers we will be disappointed. Not every service user will want to become a co-researcher, nor should they be made to do so! If you remember the discussion on ethics it was seen as an imperative that service user co-researchers should be volunteers not conscripts. The legitimacy of service users comes not from their representativeness but from their personal experience, their perspective on the condition or service under investigation. Their personal experience is likely to have a number of similarities, or touching points, to others who have used the same services, but they will not be identical. Service users are not a homogeneous group. It also needs to be remembered that academic researchers are also not a homogeneous group as exemplified by the different positions they take on knowledge claims and how the world can be known. We would not ask for a professional researcher to be representative although we would expect them to display integrity with the methods they use and the conclusions they reach. In a similar way we do not expect service users to be representative, but when they are involved in a research project we would expect them to act with integrity, sharing their experience for the benefit of the research.

❖ 'The usual suspects'

A special case of the representativeness argument is the derogatory way in which some service users are put down as representing 'the usual suspects'. This view suggests that there are a small group of acceptable service users who get asked to represent the service user perspective at all events, whether it is a council meeting, a hospital consultative committee or to become a co-researcher. This group of people are often seen to be 'cherry picked' because they will not 'rock the boat' or upset the status quo. At the extreme this represents a blatant form of tokenism, where there is an illusion of participation but no real opportunity to challenge the locus of power or even willingness to consider alternative perspectives. This special case of representativeness is as spurious as it is inappropriate.

This suggests that it is important for lead researchers to remove or reduce as many barriers as possible. These barriers may include: venues, time, reward and payment, accessibility, language to be used and to offer the opportunity to be a co-researcher as widely as possible to ensure the maximum number of potential co-researchers can consider whether this is a role they could undertake or not.

It is also important when considering what tasks you are asking service users to undertake in a research project. Thus, it may be appropriate for one service user to become a member of the research reference or advisory group who feels comfortable and able to express themselves in meetings to professional researchers, other stakeholders and commissioners. Another service user may perceive such a role as boring or may only wish to become involved in the interviews and data analysis. In situations where service users become members of the advisory or reference group the lead researcher needs to consider whether the group identifies an individual who will support them in understanding the issues under discussion and facilitating their input to such meetings. This may require a pre-meeting to review the paperwork and to relate that to the research whilst identifying any service user perspectives or issues on the papers under discussion. It is potentially unethical, poor practice and research limiting to encourage service users to contribute to a research project without ensuring that contribution can be heard and incorporated into the project.

There are two other issues that should be considered at this stage in relation to the recruitment of potential service user co-researchers; one involves the training of service user co-researchers and the other the reimbursement and reward of co-researchers which was covered in Chapter 3.

In seeking to recruit service user researchers it is important to consider the development of a person specification like the one below. We are all familiar with person specifications and job descriptions as providing information about potential employment, identifying minimum job attributes and necessary qualifications to be considered for the post. Such job descriptions help service users to consider whether they have the requisite skills, knowledge and experience to become service user co-researchers (see Figure 5.1).

The above person specification is by necessity broad as it seeks to be inclusive, although it does highlight certain key issues. It highlights the need for service user co-researcher to be service users in the field they are researching. It is inappropriate to think of, for example, older physically disabled people to be employed as service user co-researchers in a project on the experiences of young people with cancer. They may be very good researchers but they could not claim to be service users of the services being investigated. It is good practice to identify the purpose of the role for which you are seeking to recruit service users to undertake and the key responsibilities of that role. It is also preferable to identify the timescale, as far as possible, that they you are seeking to engage co-researchers for. Different tasks may have different timescales and it may not be necessary for everyone to sign up for everything. It is also an opportunity to begin to clarify issues about what people will be expected to do, what levels of qualification they require and some of the initial expectations, like completing the training, maintaining anonymity and confidentiality, the levels of reward and reimbursement for expenses.

Training of service user co-researchers

As already noted, it would be unethical to expect service users, or any other member of the public volunteering to be a service user co-researcher, to automatically have the knowledge, skills and expertise to be a service user co-researcher without any training. For those service users who are new to research it should be a mandatory requirement before they take part in a research project to successfully complete a research training course. It should also be noted that researchers may also require training to work with service users in helping them to recognize power differentials and to develop anti-oppressive practices to facilitate service user co-researchers developing the necessary skills. Researchers need to be able to work in a manner which emphasizes involvement, collaboration and partnership. It is a waste of everyone's time, not to say unethical, for a researcher to set up a project involving service user co-researchers and then failing to maximize the benefits of those recruited for this purpose.

Before any training of service user co-researchers takes place it is important to consider questions about venue, timing, length of session, team building, research activities to be undertaken, frequency of sessions, purpose of session, pedagogical principles underpinning the training, how the training will be evaluated and quality assured and any other supplementary training that may be required during the research. All this needs to be considered and planned before the training begins. It is also important not to be too fixed by any programme and to know when it is important to deviate from the programme and when it is not. Some training courses may cover a number of weeks whilst others may be run intensively over a long weekend. It is also likely that once the research is in progress that further training will be required. If service user co-researchers are to be involved in data analysis it is likely that the data analysis will only truly come alive when there is data to analyse and synthesize. Whilst initial training may cover general principles it is probably helpful to have further training sessions once there is research data available to link the general to the specific. In preparing such a plan it is important to consider the availability of service user co-researchers and the budget, both of which are likely to be major determinants as to which approaches are possible. Although it is possible to design an ideal training programme any research budget is unlikely to be able to fund everything and there is likely to be some form of compromise between aspirations and the resources available.

The TRUE Project (Lockey et al., 2004) sought to identify what training opportunities were available to service users who wished to develop their research skills. The project also included service users as co-researchers and conducted 36 telephone interviews of 26 active training providers and visited 6 training sites interviewing participants, trainers and commissioners and observing training taking place. From this information they concluded that research training for service users was not readily available, and what training there was tended to be specific to an individual research project. They found that service user training was most useful when it had a clear aim and purpose with real research problems and drew upon participant's experience. Importantly, they found that undertaking such training had positive benefits for service users in terms of promoting personal development and confidence. The TRUE Project (Lockey et al., 2004) also noted that training needed to be seen as more than a didactic activity where the academic researcher acts as an expert imparting knowledge to unknowing students. Instead, what was required was an educational style that takes on board adult learning principles and is more in keeping with researcher 'development' as opposed to researcher 'training'. Such an approach requires any 'trainer' to have skills in facilitation as well as expert knowledge. In many ways these skills are reflective of community development work with its emphasis upon empowerment, groupwork skills and self-development. It should be remembered that service users who are putting themselves forward to become co-researchers are likely to have had a diverse experience of compulsory education, with some who have university degrees and others for whom school was a negative experience and who left school at the first opportunity. This presents a particular challenge for research trainers who need to be able to demystify research terminology, and present their information in an intellectually honest manner that is neither demeaning nor overly challenging. Service users, like any of us, will not take too kindly to those they feel are talking down to them. Similarly, if it is too challenging they may just give up trying. The training or development of service users requires service users to take a risk in exposing themselves to their fellow 'students' and it is the responsibility of the 'trainer' to ensure that this is undertaken in a safe environment where mistakes can be seen as potential learning opportunities.

Lockey et al. (2004) also commented that typically service users were not paid for undertaking the training whilst researchers and trainers were. You will have noted from the job description in Figure 5.1 that it was suggested service users would receive payment for undertaking the training. This seems only just as the costs of training need to be included within any research bid. Why should service users be expected to give up of their time for free whilst others do not? If we wish to value the co-researchers we need to be seen to be doing this from the start of the research project. Also, service users should not be out of pocket and any expenses, like travelling costs or caring responsibilities, should be factored into the reimbursement strategy for the project.

Secondly, the quality of the research project will ultimately depend on the quality of the co-researchers. If we do not invest in their training or development we cannot be surprised if we end up with an inferior product. Service user co-researchers should only be expected to undertake research activities which are commensurate with their abilities and for which there is evidence they have the ability to undertake and which they feel they have ability to undertake successfully. One way of ensuring the quality of service user co-researchers is for any training to be externally accredited; this also has the advantage for service users of providing a qualification that they can either use as confirmation of their skills or as part of a future job application. Nevertheless, as noted above, there are very few opportunities for service users to access research method courses. This creates a problem in that it becomes doubly difficult to provide a bespoke research methods course that will meet the research project needs and also provide the service user co-researchers with a recognized research methods qualification. University quality assurance systems for new programmes are noted for their lack of responsiveness and long lead-in times, making them largely unsuitable for this process. Such a programme is also likely to mean that any research project takes longer whilst the planning, mapping and approval of the course against external benchmarks and quality standards is undertaken. One example of such an individualized programme was the University of Lancaster run Certificate in Social Research Methods for Older People (Leamy and Clough, 2006) and this is identified further in the following practice example.

Practice Example

Leamy and Clough (2006) describe how older people (60 years and over) became involved as researchers in a research study called 'Housing Decisions in Older Age'. The research team believed that providing university-validated training was the best way to ensure that older people with no research experience could develop the necessary research skills to undertake the project interviews and for their results to be taken seriously by policy makers. To this end they developed a Certificate in Research Methods which was validated at level one of an undergraduate degree and weighted at 40 units. The course aimed to provide a theoretical and practical understanding and competence in interviewing skills.

Following the completion of the Certificate in Research Methods the older researchers wanted further research training and a further two courses were developed around the themes of 'Research Networks' and 'Research Skills for Older People' which involved two sessions per week over a five-week period with assignments. The course programme included:

An Older People's Research Network?

1. *What determines the current research agenda concerning later life*
2. *Research and key decisions on health and social care policy affecting older people*
3. *Older people as researchers*
4. *Current research projects in the North West related to later life and older people*
5. *An older people's research network? Review and next steps*

Two assignments: one to provide key points why an academic partner should be chosen for a study on age discrimination, and two, to develop one idea for a research project.

Older People as Researcher: Potential, Practicalities and Pitfalls

1. *Developing a research proposal*
2. *(1) Telephone interviewing*
   (2) Qualitative data analysis revisited
3. *Developing a research proposal (2) Assessing research proposals*
   Assessment criteria of different organizations
   Further work on individual or group research proposals
4. *(1) Setting out your stall*
   (2) Developing a research proposal
5. *Construction of an interview schedule*
   Assessment to consist of notes written to the title 'Reflection on writing a research proposal' – 2–3,000 words.

In this practice example it was important, both for the research process and for the validity of the research from a research commissioner's perspective, that the older people researchers should have an externally validated research qualification. Leamy and Clough (2006) also highlight what this group of older people learned by doing; they discovered how to interview and what research is about from the activity of undertaking research. In this case learning by doing did not just include older people discovering about research from their own activity but also from theory and from experienced researchers. If we wish service user co-researchers to become research competent we need to ensure that not only do we provide potential co-researchers with opportunities to develop the practical skills but also to understand the theory that underpins the skills and informs the research process. To just teach a skill without theory is to treat potential service user co-researchers as instruments and to negate the potential they have to contribute to the research process. To just include theory without the opportunity to develop research skills is to promote research as an abstract conceptual activity and to lose an opportunity for developing a deeper level of understanding by bringing both theory and practice together. This does mean that those who seek to include service users as co-researchers in research projects will need to build in sufficient time to ensure that the co-researchers have had the opportunities to develop the pre-requisite skills but also to understand how, and why, such skills were necessary to address the research question. Such a process also needs to include some form of quality assurance, whether this includes passing assignments, as in the case of Leamy and Clough (2006), or some other form of assessment. It would be highly unethical to set service use co-researchers free on other potentially vulnerable people if there has not been some assessment made that the service user co-researchers were competent to complete the task. There is not a great deal written specifying the pedagogical underpinnings of service user co-researcher development or of the content of particular research courses for service users and how they are assessed; this represents a gap in our knowledge and understanding.

Literature review

The literature review can be undertaken at different times in the research and it has been included after the training as it would be a dereliction of duty to imagine service user co-researchers should be asked to contribute to a literature review before they had any research training. It is also accepted that there is likely to have been an initial literature review undertaken in the research bid. For our purposes:

> A literature review is an assessment of existing knowledge – both empirical and theoretical – relating to our research topic, issue or question. (Becker and Bryman, 2004: 69)

The purpose of a literature review is to check what has been written about the area of research previously, to identify gaps in the existing knowledge base, to highlight concepts and ideas that have been used to help illuminate the area of study and which at a later stage may be particularly helpful in interrogating the research data. A literature review can provide 'clues' as to which aspects of the data to highlight and may provide some 'pegs' on which to hang ideas (Becker and Bryman, 2004).

In working with service user co-researchers lead researchers need to take the opportunity to use their expertise in the literature review. Service user co-researchers can be involved in the identification of potential documentary sources of information. Lead researchers can undertake 'thought showers' with service user co-researchers to identify as many different sources of documentary evidence that could be used in the specific research question. Service user co-researchers may know of specific studies or projects that could be useful in informing the research. They may also know of others who have been involved in research studies or may have been research respondents in other people's research studies.

Having identified a source of reports, articles and books it is important that these are read with an agreed series of questions to identify their messages, credibility and validity for the research under question. This is an attempt to ensure a standardized systematic structure to the interrogation of the documentary evidence in order to reduce the risk that a study is either overlooked or given undue weight. It is possible to draw up a set of questions with the co-researchers to refer to when analysing or examining documentary sources. It is also possible to use or adapt a proprietary appraisal system like CASP (critical appraisal skills programme) as developed by the Public Health Research Unit (www.phru.nhs.ac/Pages/PHD/resource.htm accessed 15/02/2008) with individual appraisal questionnaire forms for qualitative studies, systematic reviews, case control studies and random control trials. Likewise (Newman et al., 2005) have developed a similar tool for social work practitioners to appraise quality and to decide whether a research study is sufficiently credible and trustworthy to justify its inclusion. Most of these systems include initial screening questions to help the researcher decide whether they should continue with the article or not. The types of questions a service user co-researcher appraisal system might include are:

- Was there a clear statement of aims?
- Was the research methodology appropriate?
- Is it worthwhile carrying on reading this? (If you answered no to either question you should stop reading the research.)
- What were the assumptions behind the research?
- Was the data collection method appropriate?
- What alternative explanations were considered?

- Are the research results justified by the data collection?
- Are the messages of this research useful for our study?

Having completed the appraisal questionnaires these have to be critically synthesized into a literature review. This is likely, but not necessarily so, to require an academic researcher to do the writing. If this is the case the service user co-researchers should be asked to consider both the critical appraisal questionnaires and a draft of the literature review and to whether they feel it has captured the messages from the studies.

Barriers to involvement

> ### Reflexive Questions
>
> ✳ Imagine you are a service user of health and social care services, what barriers can you imagine that might make it difficult for you to participate in a research project?

Amongst the barriers you might have included in your list:

- Research is only for those with a university degree.
- My caring duties are too prohibitive.
- I'll be shown up as stupid.
- I won't be able to get to the training or research sites.
- I won't be able to get in the building.
- I can't get to the research sites.
- I won't be able to understand the big words.
- I wasn't very good with maths at school.
- I'm not very good at reading or writing.
- I haven't got the confidence to interview people.
- I don't know what research is.
- I don't expect it will make any difference whether I get involved or not.
- The payment rules are too complex.
- My medical condition fluctuates, making it difficult for me to commit.

You may have identified all the potential barriers identified above and possibly a few that aren't included. It is interesting to look at some of the themes indentified in the barriers above. There are a number of barriers that revolve around academic or intellectual ability: issues to do with having a degree, poor performance in mathematics, reading or writing. These barriers are both real and unreal. It all depends on the research activities to be undertaken by the co-researchers. McClimens et al. (2007: 117) observe in relation to people with learning disabilities:

> 'Doing research' involves a multiplicity of tasks, some making more intellectual demands than others, and expecting people with learning disabilities to be involved in all stages of the research may not be practicable; indeed, it may even be unethical if it places unreasonable demands upon some individuals.

As we mentioned earlier, it would not be right to ask co-researchers to undertake tasks they had neither the skills nor abilities to undertake. There are research tasks which go beyond the skill levels of those without research training of a higher order. However, this is different from suggesting that some of this group of service users, if given appropriate training and support, would not be able to undertake research tasks. It is also possible that there may be other tasks, such as: membership of a steering group or helping to advise on questions that this group of people would be able to contribute towards the research process.

Other barriers are concerned with caring duties or access to buildings or research sites. These, along with issues like timing of the training or research visits, are practical questions. If researchers and research commissioners want to involve service users they need to consider how important this is to their research and in certain cases build in funding to cover the cost of paying for a carer's cover which may include child care or domiciliary support costs for an older relative. The research proposal should also have considered the need to include travel costs or identified support workers who can transport service users to research meetings and research sites. Associated with this is also the question of the complexity of payment rules which have been discussed previously. The payment rules are complex and it is important for lead researchers to ensure service users are not financially exploited and receive their due reward for their involvement.

Similarly it is important to consider the timings of research meetings, or research interviews, so that they are not exclusionary. In deciding upon timings for research training and meetings these should be guided by a discussion with the service user co-researchers rather than assuming that everyone is available during traditional working hours. However, when you are considering accessing research sites the research respondent's consideration of timing needs to be driven by when the research respondents will be available. This should be established as early in the research as possible to ensure all are aware of the likely time commitments the research will require.

There is also a knowledge and confidence barrier: 'I haven't got the confidence to interview people'; 'I'd be shown up as stupid'; and 'I don't know what research is'.

This barrier can be addressed from the start of the research process with clear and easy to read/view/listen to information available for all to consider whether they wish to become a service user co-researcher. Alongside this should also be an identification of how service user co-researchers will be given the opportunity to develop skills to become competent interviewers and how these new skills will be developed in ways which focus on strengths, develop knowledge and demystify what research is.

The next barrier: 'I don't expect it will make any difference whether I get involved or not', is both an example of apathy and realism. Apathy, in that if no one tries to make a difference, issues of service users will not be heard. As has been previously noted there is no guarantee that research will make a difference; once a research report is published and is in the public domain the matter is out of the hands of the research team. There is no easy to specify formula which indicates which research reports will make a difference and which will not. It is, however, essential that academic researchers are honest about this from the very beginning of the research process, avoiding unrealistic expectations and any subsequent disappointment or disillusionment.

The last barrier is of a different order, and the uncertain trajectory of certain illnesses, like multiple sclerosis or cancer, may make it difficult for some potential service user co-researcher to commit themselves for a long period. This though doesn't mean that they cannot be involved in the research but that research managers will need to be creative in how they use co-researchers and may need to recruit more than first thought to cover the situation where individual illnesses may limit participation.

In this section we have considered a number of barriers to involvement. In considering these barriers we have shown that they are not insurmountable but require some prior planning and consideration. If this is done there is no reason why these barriers cannot be ameliorated and why there cannot be meaningful service user involvement as co-researchers without over-claiming or under-claiming what can be achieved.

Establishment of a reference or steering group

It is accepted practice for research projects to establish a reference or steering group. The two terms are often used interchangeably, a reference group tends to imply a group the researchers will use to check things out with whilst a steering group suggests a more active involvement in setting the direction of the research. In reality they both tend to cover the same range of topics, including: an update on the research so far, problem sharing and resolution, tracking progress and identifying next steps. This means that reference or steering groups need to include those who can help or have influence in dealing with this range of topics. This means that they may include research commissioner representatives, an independent academic representative, a representative of the agencies involved in the research, two service user representatives and research team members. It is important that we do not ask service users to appear in such meetings by themselves and to ensure that they are supported. This support may include transport and costs to attend at an accessible venue but should also include an agenda beforehand and an opportunity to find out more information about any item that is on the agenda. To maximize the contribution of service user co-researchers it is necessary to make sure that they have the appropriate support and tools. A further requirement is that the chairs of such groups have the skills necessary to facilitate inclusive discussions in plain English (or whatever is the first language of the service users), are able to avoid discussions getting bogged down in jargon and can accentuate the strengths and positives that service user co-researchers bring to such arenas.

Practice Example

For a research project to promote 'Best Practice' with D/deaf service users and their sensory disability social work teams we established a reference group. This group consisted of D/deaf service user, social work managers, the research team and a commissioner from the Royal National Institute for the Deaf People (RNID) and a representative from the DH who was partially sighted. In order to promote communication within this group there was also a sign language interpreter, an audio loop system and as there was a lip-reader in the group we also had to ensure we spoke clearly whilst I also needed to trim my moustache and beard to ensure the lip-reader could see my lips clearly! A number of the hearing members of the group were proficient in British Sign Language (BSL) but if the meeting were to be conducted in BSL the other hearing members, lip-reader, hearing aid wearer and the partially sighted member would not be able to contribute. Also, if our partially sighted member, as was his usual standard, was to bang the table to signal he wanted to speak, the deaf members of the group would not be able to hear. Given the range of communication needs we spent most of the first meeting trying to establish a protocol that would allow everyone to be able to communicate. It was also necessary to ensure our partially sighted member had his papers in an electronic version early so that they could be transposed to Braille prior to the meeting and that arrangements were also made for his guide dog to be fed and watered. Paying attention to the detail gives service users the message that they and their contributions are valued. (Young et al., 2004)

Development of the research tools

This may be included in the training of service users or may be undertaken as a separate activity. As mentioned in Chapter 1, one of the strengths of involving service users in research is the opportunity to check that questions are relevant, meaningful and speak to the issues that are important to service users. This means that questionnaire questions, focus groups or interview schedules are worded in such a way that they reflect the needs of research commissioners and are understandable to service users. This is also an opportunity to consider the sequencing of questions, potential answers, research venues and to identify strategies to engage harder to reach service user groups. This type of work is often best done using groupwork skills focusing on learning by doing and actively engaging the service user co-researchers. This entails acknowledging the expertise of the service user co-researchers and ensuring there is air time for their contributions to be heard. This can be hard when service user co-researchers want different things and will demand that the lead researcher, or whoever is facilitating the session, is able to manage disagreements. Disagreements are not inherently bad and may be useful in further refining and identifying questions that may be interpreted in more than one way. It should be remembered that it would be highly unlikely for any research team, whether they include service user co-researchers or not, to always agree on what is included in the research instruments.

Being involved in the development of the research instruments helps co-researchers to own the research. Ownership of the research is essential for ensuring that service user co-researchers understand the importance of each question and are able to offer further explanation if required. Ownership of the research instrument development is likely to result in further benefits throughout the research process. If you have been involved at this early stage you are more likely to want to continue to be involved in taking part in the data analysis to know the responses to the questions that you helped develop.

Summary

This chapter has taken a more practical stance towards service user involvement in research than previous chapters. In particular it has highlighted issues concerning research conception, service user recruitment, including a job specification for service user co-researchers, the training of service user co-researchers with an example from a project with older people. The chapter has also identified potential barriers to research involvement and how these practical and methodological obstacles can be addressed or ameliorated. There has also been a discussion of the operation of reference or steering groups and opportunities for service user co-researchers in peer reviewing and commissioning boards.

The chapter has highlighted the significance of promoting the ownership by service user co-researchers and the development of research tools. In seeking to involve service user co-researchers the message is very clear, the sooner the better. The longer this is left, the less likely service user co-researchers will own the process and the less likely that they will be willing to contribute beyond what is required. This is not to deny that service user co-researchers can, and do, contribute to different elements in the research process but that the sooner you are involved and are able to make a contribution the more you will feel you have a stake in the outcome. As this chapter has shown, this is often easier to say than do and requires extra effort, considerations and resources to be undertaken successfully.

(It should also be noted that the recommended reading for this chapter is included at the end of the next chapter as both these chapters are inextricably linked parts of the same process.)

Figure 5.1	Job Description for a Mental Health Service User Co-researcher

Job Purpose

The purpose of this role is to be an integral part of a research team investigating service user experiences of using the services provided by Midtown Mental Health Outreach Team.

Responsibilities

- To successfully complete the research training supplied by Dr Brown and colleagues.
- To work with fellow co-researchers, Dr Brown and the advisory group in developing research questions, interviewing service users, recording interviews, participating in data analysis and contributing to the final report.
- To attend meetings, briefings and contribute to the research project which is to be completed within 12 months.
- To retain confidentiality in relation to the research information and maintain the anonymity of those interviewed.
- To participate in the dissemination of the research results.
- To advise Dr Brown of any conflicts of interest or reasons why they are unable to undertake any part of the research project.

Person Specification

Qualifications

The successful candidate should:	Essential / Desirable
No formal qualifications required	

Background & Experience

The successful candidate should:	
■ Have experience of mental health services as a service user ■ Have experience of working in a team	Essential Desirable

Knowledge

The successful candidate should have demonstrable knowledge of and:	
■ Have an understanding of mental health services, practitioners and service users	Essential
■ Be committed to working in an anti-discriminatory way	Essential

Skills & Competencies

The successful candidate should demonstrate:	
■ Good communication skills	Essential
■ A potential and willingness to develop research skills	Essential
■ An ability to respond to challenging tasks	Essential
■ An ability to see commitments through	Essential

Expenses and Payments

All reasonable expenses will be covered including e.g. attending training, visiting research sites analysing data and disseminating results. All co-researchers will be paid £100 on completion of the training, £50 for helping develop the research tools, £15 for each interview completed and £30 for supporting the analysis of the data and writing up the report.

(This exemplar from mental health services will be followed through in this and the next chapter to allow the reader to follow an example through; however, it would be quite easy to change the exemplar to fit other service user groups.)

6 Practical Issues and Stumbling Blocks: From Data Analysis to Dissemination

Introduction

This chapter builds on from the work of the previous chapter in following through the 'how' of service user co-researcher involvement, using the research process as a device to highlight key issues and challenges. In this chapter we focus on the issues associated with data collection, analysing data, writing the report and disseminating the findings.

Reflexive Questions

✳ Before beginning to examine some of the issues for service user co-researchers in relation to data collection you might wish to consider what types of issues you think there are for service user co-researchers. In particular you might like to think about practical, emotional and academic issues.

Data collection

The data collection part of the research process involves the period in which the researchers gather their research data; this is most likely to involve the completion of questionnaires, semi-structured interviews or focus groups, but may also include the recording of respondents' life stories, the use of vignettes or even a ghost shopper exercise. Vignettes are often short exemplars from which respondents are then asked their views about what should happen next. A ghost shopper exercise is where a service user co-researcher would be given a task to find out how easy or difficult it is to gain access or information about a particular service. They are provided with a 'normal story' and as such provide information as to how service users are normally treated and how easy, or difficult, it is for them to gain the requisite information or service.

Practical Example

A voluntary child care agency wanted to find out how each of their new centres dealt with child protection referrals and whether these were in keeping with agency policy. As I was already working with a group of young people who had experience of the child safeguarding system we jointly identified a 'normal' scenario. This scenario was designed to check out the agency's policy in relation to: allowing young people to make anonymous calls, to tell their story at their own pace and for the caller to feel that they would be welcome to call again and to make an appointment to see a worker. Having agreed the scenario we role-played it between ourselves amending as necessary until we had a script that everyone felt comfortable with. Following on from this we then arranged a date and a venue which had a number of phones so that the young people could call each centre at roughly the same time with the same scenario. Having done this, we compared how each centre had responded. Most of the centres responded very positively, with the young people stating they would have been willing to share personal information with the person on the other end of the line, except in three cases: one where the young person felt they were not being listened to; one who asked the young person to contact the local social services or Childline; and another where we were not able to get through at all. When the results were communicated to the organization they developed an action plan to meet the shortcomings identified by the ghost shopper exercise.

❖ Practical issues

Before data collection commences there is a need to consider some practical points, beginning with the venue(s) and timing where the research is to take place. If it is to be a telephone survey then amongst the important issues to consider will be the noise levels, the requisite number of available telephones and whether the telephones can be wired to record the research interview. Some service users may prefer hands-free sets so that they can record the interview schedule if need be. It will also be important to ensure that the interviewers have at least two pens. Pens are most likely to run out of ink when it most difficult to replace them!

If the interviews or questionnaires are to be undertaken at a service user venue, for example a day centre, the research team will need to consider when they attend. It may seem rather simplistic, but it is no good attending the day centre when it is most convenient for the research team if the day centre is closed or when only a few people are in attendance. The research team also need to consider transport arrangements to ensure everyone can get to and from the day centre. In using buildings, it is also necessary to consider that where any interviews take place to ensure the safety of the service user co-researchers and research respondents. There is a balance to be drawn between safety and confidentiality, which needs to be considered before the research team begin any interviews and a recording 'in and out' system so that all the research team visiting any site can be accounted for at all times. It is also good practice to set up a research room with refreshments where the service user co-researchers can congregate in between their interviews. There may also be a need to consider whether service user co-researchers undertake interviews in pairs or individually and issues of matching may become important. Certainly undertaking an interview in a pair may provide a greater confidence and security for the interviewers but it may feel oppressive to the interviewee. Similarly, for some interview situations it may be important for interviewees to be interviewed by someone of a similar gender in relation to issues of sexual dysfunction, or the same sexual orientation when considering issues of gay, lesbian and trans-sexual mental health, or of the same ethnic grouping or religious persuasion when considering older people's needs for day care services. There are no hard and fast rules here, but what is required is that the research team consider the issue of how best they can promote a facilitative relationship that is most likely to allow any research respondent to feel they can be honest and share their views and experiences. If the interviewees do not feel comfortable, or have trust in the competence of the service user co-researchers, they will not be fully co-operative and more likely to ensure the interview is over as quickly as possible. This needs to be tempered against the need for service user co-researchers to feel confident as they are more likely to perform better if they are not unduly worried, uncomfortable or at risk. It is appropriate, and to be expected, that they should feel a degree of anxiety due to adrenalin which can help them to perform better, but if they become too aroused it will inhibit their performance. At the end of the interview it is important to de-brief the service user co-researchers to check if anything needs to be changed prior to next interview, or whether some emotional discomfort or pain has been raised that requires attention.

These measures become more complicated if you are seeking to undertake research with harder to reach groups, like people who misuse drugs and who are not using statutory services. By definition this group may be 'hanging out' in areas that are harder to provide surveillance. Whilst service user co-researchers or those who used to be drug dependent are recruited because they know where such activities take place, there is also a need to remember that the lead researcher has a duty of care in relation to the service user co-researchers. Thus, in engaging in such activities it is necessary to consider how co-researchers could attract attention and be extracted if they find themselves in an uncomfortable, illegal or dangerous situation. This might include the use of mobile phones or panic alarms. The use of such preventative measures will need to have been covered in the training to ensure that everyone knows what to do if an alarm is activated. Interviews in such situations should be undertaken in pairs if there is any concern whatsoever about the safety of the service user co-researchers. It is also desirable that if a situation becomes assessed as too high a risk the interview is abandoned. Again, if interviews are undertaken it is very important that the service user co-researchers are able to check in after each interview; a local meeting point should also be identified as an opportunity for de-briefing at the end of the session.

❖ Process issues

When an interview schedule is to be handled by more than one service user co-researcher, it is vital that the same guidelines are followed by each interviewer to ensure maximum comparability. Such instructions need to be explicit and should be printed and include information as to who the interviewer is, what is the purpose of the interview and which organization the service user co-researcher represents. Within this initial guide the service user co-researcher also needs to remind the research respondent about their rights to confidentiality and anonymity, even if this has been covered prior to the interview taking place.

Practical Example

Good morning/afternoon/evening. I am .... from the Mental Health Research Project at the University of Salport. We are conducting a survey on behalf of the local council and Midtown Area Health Authority to find out what people think of the mental health outreach services in the town. A number of members attending the Midtown Day Centre have been selected for interview in this survey. You have been selected and this is an opportunity for you to 'have a say' about how you rate the current local services and whether there are any other services you would like to see developed. The questions have been drawn up by other mental outreach service users who are actively involved in the research. Your agreement to take part would be greatly appreciated.

Everything you say will be treated confidentially. No names will be attached to any information you provide and you can withdraw, without any effect upon the services you receive. You can also decide to miss a question if you wish.

> *The interview will last about 45 minutes and if you agree, it will be taped to ensure accuracy.*
> *Can you confirm that you received the letter about this research and that this is your signed consent agreeing to take part in the study?*
> *Would it be convenient to start the interview now?*
> *(Based on Simmons, 2001: 100)*

If the interview includes closed questions it may be easier for some of these to have the potential answers on a prompt card. Where the interview schedule includes open questions it is important to record the information on a tape or digital recorder. If the service user co-researcher has to take copious notes it is likely that they will lose the thread of what is happening and risk annoying their research respondent by their frequent gaps. This is particularly important in telephone interviewing where silence can be misinterpreted as disinterest (see Figure 6.1).

The above example provides a mixture of open and closed questions with potential answers able to be circled for the closed questions, allowing faster completion of the questionnaire. Ideally the interview should be taped, but it may also be useful to quickly make some notes of the answers in case there should be any difficulties with the tape. When using a tape or digital recorder you need to make sure that the batteries are still working and that you have spare batteries should the ones in the machine not last. If intending to plug a recording machine into a wall socket you need to ensure the lead is long enough to allow the recorder to be in a central place. The choice of venue should also take into account the amount of background noise that may make the tape difficult to decode. You should also check that the machine is recording once the interview begins; many a good interview has been lost by the failure to check that the recorder is recording. If using tapes, you also need to ensure you have sufficient tapes to record all your interviewees, or if using a digital machine, that it has sufficient memory. It is also good practice to offer the research respondent the opportunity to have a transcribed record of the interview so that they can check it for accuracy. This is not always straightforward, as Barnes and Mercer (2006: 60) acknowledge when they quote Campbell and Oliver's (1996) experience, where only two out of 30 key activists took up the opportunity to 'validate' interview transcripts or read the draft manuscript. This can lead to a delay in the process. One way around this is to give respondents a cut-off date to respond, and if they have not responded by the agreed date it is assumed they are happy with the transcript. Any responses may not only affirm what has been recorded but also provide additional material. More problematic is when the interviewee suggests that the record is inaccurate and this may require further contact to re-negotiate, or the interview will have to be deemed void and not used. It may also be difficult with the harder-to-reach or stigmatized groups to be able to undertake such a process, and the research respondent should be advised that should they want to have a transcript then an alternative system will need to be established.

At the end of the interview the co-researcher needs to thank the research respondent for their time and advise them what is to happen to their information and how they will be able to find out the results and recommendations of the study. All too often research neglects to inform research respondents of findings and treats them like 'cannon fodder'. It is thus essential that research that seeks to empower service users does not fall into the same trap.

Where service users are also interviewing staff, there is an important power dynamic that needs to be considered. From the service user co-researcher perspective staff members are likely to be seen as powerful figures that can control their right of entry to a particular service: to ease this worry, if possible, service user co-researchers should not be asked to interview staff members who deal directly with their treatment or service provision. It is also worth considering whether every staff member should be interviewed by two service user researchers to provide support to each other in this power reversal.

After each research session service user co-researchers should be encouraged to complete a research log, or diary, including their field notes of that research session, reflective comments on the process and any issues they wish to raise with the rest of the research team. A typical research diary could include the following headings/themes:

- Date, venue, time and length of interview.
- Details of research respondent (gender, age range, diagnosed condition, length of time used Midtown Day services, etc.).
- What worked well in the research interview?
- What needs to be looked at next time?
- Key messages from the respondent.
- How does this compare with previous interviewees?
- How does this affect my understanding of the mental health outreach services in Midtown?
- Issues to be raised with the research team.

As previously noted, there is no a priori reason why service user co-researchers cannot be involved in any aspect of the research, but this should be determined by the level of their research skills and knowledge matched against their degree of confidence and comfort in facing an unknown situation. The importance of meaningful training to undertake this role cannot be overemphasized.

Analysing the data

Many research studies, and possibly all service evaluations, require both qualitative and quantitative data and will include both closed and open questions. By implication, this means that a range of methods will be required to analyse the data.

❖ *Closed questions*

Having collected the data, it is important to make sense of it. Depending on the techniques being used, service user co-researchers can have a larger or smaller part in the process. If the research data has been collected using an interview schedule with closed questions, the data can be written in such a way that is easy to translate to a computer package for undertaking statistical tests, or it may be needed to be added in manually to a statistical programme like SPSS. It is also possible to provide training sessions on the coding and categorization of quantitative and qualitative data. Statistical analysis is often seen as one of the most mysterious, mystifying and frightening aspects of a social research survey. This is understandable, as many statistical techniques to manipulate and interrogate the data are likely to be beyond the skill levels of service user co-researchers. Issues such as probability, statistical significance, t-tests, power, correlations, criterion validity, log linear analysis, multiple regression and more advanced mathematically oriented statistical approaches will be beyond the ability of the average service user co-researcher.

Whilst advanced statistical approaches are likely to be outside the skill set of service user co-researchers, this is not the same as claiming that service user co-researchers cannot be taught basic descriptive statistics. It should also be noted that this lack of statistical capacity is not necessarily a criticism of service user co-researchers, as research teams often include a specialist in this area to act on behalf of the team. Not all lead researchers will be proficient in all aspects of research and will put teams together with the requisite quantitative and qualitative skills to meet the needs of the topic under research. It should also be remembered that the intellectual effort in dealing with the mysteries of data analysis and statistics should be equivalent to the intellectual effort spent in conceptualizing the problem, designing the questionnaire and writing up the report (Procter, 2001).

❖ *Open questions*

With the use of open questions or more semi-structure interview techniques the initial data will need to be transcribed. There are now a number of computer packages that will transcribe spoken language; however, computer software packages like Via Voce need the user to have used them regularly so that the package can pick up the individual speech patterns with a high degree of accuracy. This is likely to mean that they will be of limited use to a service user co-researcher project, as even if the co-researchers have spent a lot of time with a package the research respondent will not have. This means that transcriptions will either need to be undertaken by a paid copy typist, or there may even be a service user co-researcher who has such skills.

Once the data is transcribed, the research team then needs to begin to code the data. Again, there are now a number of computer assisted qualitative packages on the market, which include QSR NUD*IST or NVIVO, both of which help researchers manage the data and interrogate their ideas:

> Transcripts of interviews, descriptions and narratives can produce a lot of text. Handling such data can be disorganised and *messy*. When interpreting and recording significance, commonality, exceptions or tracking a story, it is difficult to keep in touch with all the ideas you may have about the data. You need to keep in touch with examples of the data that demonstrate those ideas and the connection between those ideas. Whether the data are in textual, audio, video, or graphic format, ideas about them nearly always relate to parts of them. In essence software seeks to maintain an easy contact between the ideas and those parts, while allowing an overview of the whole. (Lewins, 2001: 303; italics in original)

Lewins (2001: 303) provides a clear rationale for the use of computer assisted qualitative analysis, although she also notes that software learning is not the same as 'user friendliness'. So, although Lewins has identified some of the complexity for dealing with qualitative data, this again, like statistical approaches, may require a specialist to use the software. It should also be remembered that such computer packages are not a substitute for researcher analysis.

Not all analysis is done by computer and much may be done by hand. This may or, may not, be within the abilities of the co-researchers. Warren and Cook (2005) note that, having shown their volunteers two anonymized coded interview transcripts, the co-researchers decided the detailed analysis was beyond the skill and experience of the volunteers. If we go back to our example of the mental health outreach services it may be appropriate that once the interviews have been transcribed and coded and the service user co-researchers have had their research notes typed up, to organize a data analysis day to discuss the preliminary results. Such a day can begin with the sharing of findings and views with the other co-researchers and, depending on the number of co-researchers, this can be done first in pairs and then in fours before sharing as a full group using flipcharts to capture the key points. After the collection of basic information such as age, gender, etc. the interrogation of the data and first impressions needs to be collated. This collation needs to be undertaken in a structured process and from the practice questionnaire sample identified earlier this might include a flipchart containing all the answers generated by the individual questions like: '*Which sessions do you value and why?*' These should include both the names of the sessions and the reasons why they were valued. This can then allow a comparing and contrasting between day centre attendees and an opportunity to see whether sessions are valued for similar or diverse reasons. For example, groupwork sessions may be valued because of the skills of the groupworker, the attractiveness of the groupworker, the growth experienced by the service user whilst attending the sessions, or as an opportunity to get out of the house. In understanding service delivery it is imperative not only to be able to comment on what is valued but why it is valued. For example, what if the weekly 'managing depression' course is poorly attended? This may be as much to do with the timing of the session (8 am on Monday mornings), as it is to the content or delivery. Those most likely to benefit from such sessions are probably those who find it most difficult to get going in the morning. Making judgements about which programmes are valued is not the same as making judgements about the needs of those who attend the centre and how they may be met.

Having identified the answers to all the questions it is then important to look at whether there are some themes coming through. For example, it might be that those who valued groupwork wanted more of the same, and valued staff who had groupwork skills, wanted to develop skills that would increase their employment prospects. Or, conversely, those who only attended the drop-in only wanted better coffee making facilities and preferred staff that were invisible and similarly wanted an extra drop-in on a Wednesday evening so that they could watch the sport together. This is not to say that either approach is wrong, but at this point it is important to begin to see the connections between the information provided, the potential range of explanations and their possibility for conflict. It is also important to look at some of the closed questions and see again if there are any links or patterns to the open questions. For example, it might become clear that only those living within a three-mile radius visit the drop-in, and this would then raise issues about whether this is a good use of the service and raises a question about what happens to those who live outside the three-mile limit. As you can see from the above initial questions, research data can be messy and complex, requiring research teams to struggle to make sense of what the data is telling them.

At the end of each session it is important to capture the key themes from the data and also log any ideas that do not appear to add up. The data should then be re-visited as a research team to be interrogated again and in particular to look for ideas that do not match the main thrust to see if there is something being overlooked. This process can be repeated as many times as is necessary for the research team to feel confident about any statements they wish to make arising from their research data. It should be noted that we are looking neither for total agreement between the research team nor are we looking for the data to be totally consistent. Differences of interpretation between the service user co-researchers can lead to new insights, whilst it would be surprising if all outreach service users thought exactly the same. The research team also need to consider the limitations of their study. In relation to the outreach study, an important limitation might be that the researchers do not know the views of those who have been referred to the day centre but do not attend.

In open ended questions the last question is likely to provide the opportunity for respondents to give the interviewers information they have not been able to offer so far. This creates the possibility that research respondents will come up with answers or issues that the researchers have not thought about. It is important to expect the unexpected and to be willing to find answers that do not fit into your expectations.

The above represents an example of one way of interrogating the data from a research study which seeks to involve service users in the process. This process is messy, time consuming and challenging, and for some service user co-researchers such a process may be too daunting or difficult. In such circumstances other ways of including service user co-researchers includes asking them to act as a critical friend to the lead researcher. To do this the lead researcher undertakes the initial analysis and then shares the tentative findings with the service user co-researchers. The purpose of this is to check out with them their view as to the accuracy of the findings and whether the results have resonance with their experiences. This provides a check on the credibility and validity of the initial findings, and where the views are different, or opposed, this should result in a further interrogation of the data to see if it is the assumptions of the service user co-researchers that are inaccurate or the analysis of the data. It may in the end be neither of these but just reflect a difference in interpretation and should be reported as such. Having analysed the data, the next task is to identify any conclusions and recommendations.

Research report conclusions and recommendations

Before highlighting the research report it is worthwhile considering research conclusions and recommendations. These may appear back to front, but much of the research report may have been written by the time the data analysis is completed. A research report does not have to include any recommendations but will include conclusions. The conclusions from any research or evaluation should flow from the data. This can be easier to say than do. When working with any team there is always the potential for disagreement, and if we remember that the team were recruited because of their experiences as service users we should not expect that all service users will have had the same experience or think the same. In order to work with this position the lead researcher must continually analyse and synthesize the data as the research process progresses, checking out different interpretations, seeking clarification, integrating new knowledge and challenging assumptions. Any conclusions should be able to be justified by what has gone before and should be supported by the text in the research report.

Similarly, recommendations from the research should not come as a surprise at the end of the report. Like the conclusions, they should flow from what has gone before. Understandably, the recommendations are a very important part of the research for service user co-researchers. Recommendations can spell the end of a service or herald the introduction of a new one. Recommendations for change are often a major motivating factor why service users get involved in research in the first place. Service user co-researchers are often critical of current service provision and want to see change. It also needs to be remembered that lead researchers may have views about the nature and appropriateness of any service. In managing these feelings and emotions the lead researcher needs to demonstrate their powers of research leadership and facilitation to ensure the recommendations have flowed from the research. It is important to ensure that the report does not recommend anything that is not supported by the data. To engage in such practices is to undermine the research and runs the risk of allowing those who do not like the recommendations to ignore them on the grounds of bias in the research.

There are also a number of potential political questions here. Who decides if there is a disagreement? Is this done on a vote? Do you end up with a minority report? In deciding upon conclusions and recommendations the use of flipcharts can be useful to identify individual recommendations and to identify the evidence to support each one. It is then possible to see the quantity and quality of support for each one and to check if any key issues have been overlooked. This leads naturally onto writing the research report.

Writing the research report

Reflexive Questions

✳ If you were a service user co-researcher, what would you want to include within your research report? Now think of the audiences you might want to inform, does this make a difference as to how you write the report and what is included?

Writing a research report is a process, not an event. Parts of the report can be written as the research progresses. The typical research report will include acknowledgement of all those who took part, an identification of the research commissioner and any individuals who were particularly helpful, followed by substantive chapters identifying the original research question, an overview of the literature in the field, a chapter on the research methods and research tools used and their justification, a section on the data analysis and results and an identification of any conclusions or recommendations. We have already covered the literature review in Chapter 5.

In working with service user co-researchers there are a number of roles they can play in the writing-up stage of the process. Firstly, they can write parts of the report. For many service user co-researchers this is likely to be a step too far. However, they can add their reflections on what they did and learned in different parts of the report or write a chapter, or accompanying booklet, identifying those aspects of the research they found most revealing and compelling, identifying their messages for research commissioners along with any suggestions for future research. Service user co-researchers can also act as 'critical readers', providing feedback on the report's use of plain English, themes identified and recommendations.

It should also be noted that report writing is a political exercise. It cannot be assumed that research commissioners will welcome the research with open arms or that they will not want to influence what is said in the final report. This can be very frustrating for service user co-researchers and lead researchers alike, and can be seen as a threat to academic freedom, a principle which espouses that the discovery of truth should be reported without fear or favour (Homan, 1991). This can particularly be the case when the manager who commissioned the research had a particular outcome in mind; for example, in our exemplar of the mental health outreach study the research commissioner may have wanted the centre to be closed, to make a bid for further funding or to export the service to another part of the authority. It is also not unknown for managers to commission research to promote change knowing that the demand for change has come from a neutral source rather than from themselves (Easterby-Smith et al., 2002). Research commissioners may have their own reasons for commissioning research, of which the advancement of knowledge may not be the major driver.

As noted earlier, if the research findings are to be made available to the service user respondents the official report would be inappropriate for the task. This means turning the official report into an executive summary or providing an accessible summary or even a picture summary of the report. A good example of such a report is the *Benefits Barriers to Involvement – Finding Solutions* (CSCI, 2007) which includes pictures and photographs alongside explanatory text to clarify a complex issue which has significant impact for the involvement of service users in research. This may require expert help, and again service user co-researchers may either be able to write the text or comment on the accessibility of the text and appropriateness of the pictures.

As noted in the reflexive question, it is clear that different types of writing or information transmission are required for the different audiences. For some audiences writing may in itself be off-putting and alternative means of communication need to be considered. In working with D/deaf service users Young et al. (2007) used CDs of practice examples and a British Sign Language (BSL) video to share the key results with D/deaf service users. In these times it is also possible to consider podcasts, webpages or other electronic means to publicize the research results. If the research is to reach a variety of audiences a variety of approaches, both in the written and non-written communication styles, need to be considered and used where appropriate. Service user co-researchers can be asked to help identify the most accessible format for the different audiences.

The research does not finish with the completion of the research report. Most researchers, and this is as likely to be true of service user co-researchers as academic researchers, want to see their research make an impact, whether this is as part of a contribution to knowledge or in the form of more tangible service provision. In our previous example of the day centre this might be translated into a new way of undertaking research, a change in the opening times, a re-ordering of the services on offer or the development of a participative management committee. Whilst none of this can be assumed, and definitely not guaranteed, it is imperative at the end to consider how the research messages can best be publicized beyond the research commissioners and those participating in the research. This may include a presentation to local managers, the organization of a conference, contact with the local press, presentation of papers at conferences and the writing of articles both about the research process and the research findings.

All of these activities potentially require further training and development of the service user co-researchers. For instance, if you arrange to meet with senior managers to present your findings it is important to find out how much time you have got and plan appropriately. Senior managers are often recruited because of their abilities to influence and manage communications so it is important to make best use of the limited time available. Service users in general, and in this case service user co-researchers, can be very powerful in presenting their own case. However, this can backfire if it is not managed and presented well. This might entail the service user co-researchers reflecting on what they want from the meeting, and if this includes some commitment, to be informed of any changes to build this into the presentation. Members might each take one set of recommendations and highlight how these can be traced from the report and how they contribute to the whole. This will require prior rehearsal to ensure that any key messages are delivered in a way that the co-researchers can feel that they have done their best to ensure their messages are more likely to be heard. Such meetings can be very useful, especially if it is possible to obtain from the senior managers a commitment to send a copy of the agency's response or action plan to the research team.

Having identified a research dissemination strategy for the research there is then the issue of any academic or professional trade journal article that arises out of the research. Issues about authorship and the use of real names have previously been discussed in Chapter 3 in our review of ethical issues. The writing of international peer reviewed journal articles is unlikely to be within the ambit of most service user co-researchers. This often requires a particular style and nature of writing that takes time to develop, even for academics, and is likely to be unfamiliar to service user co-researchers. For those service user co-researchers who have been involved in a number of research projects and are developing a research career, such writing skills can be developed in conjunction with more experienced writers. Professional trade journal articles tend to be much shorter, are directed at a different audience and are often more descriptive where it is more likely that service user co-researchers' contributions will be more welcome. Publications also raise the original agreement with the research commissioner, which is likely to contain a clause that only allows publication in the public arena following commissioner agreement. It is also good practice to share any article with the agency or agencies in which the research has been conducted. This can be difficult to achieve if the commissioner or agency decision makers consider the research is critical of them or their agencies. Such events may require some skilful negotiations to avoid either an article being blocked from publication or resulting in publication of an article that is so neutered that it loses its impact. Academic freedom and the management of commissioner and research site interests can be uneasy bedfellows.

There is also a growing place for service user co-researchers in conference presentations. The Joint Social Work Education Committee (JSWEC) annual conference contains service user representatives on its planning committee, involves service users in chairing conference sessions and encourages service user presentations. Likewise INVOLVE has a bi-annual conference which promotes public involvement in public health, health and social care research and encourages all those involved, service user researchers and academics, to present papers, workshops or posters. Such venues provide opportunities for the service user co-researchers to gain exposure and recognition for their research skills and to meet others with similar interests. Again, the writing of conference abstracts and the presentation of papers or workshops requires practice and training, but these are skills that can be learned.

Activities like these also raise certain questions as to when a research project actually ends. There is the official end of the research project when the research team hand over their final deliverable, the research report. However, as noted above, this may be a sliding ending if there are meetings or conferences to organize, findings to disseminate and the potential for longer involvement if papers are to be written and presentations to be made at national or international conferences. These extra activities also raise the issue of funding, which needs to be considered by the research team in the original research bid and by any potential service user co-researcher who wishes to be involved. Or, it may lead to the joint submission of another research proposal and the start of a new research project!

Conclusions

This chapter has completed the research cycle begun in the previous chapter. In particular we have highlighted issues concerned with data collection, analysing the data, reaching conclusions and recommendations and writing up the research report and disseminating the findings. In order to make these processes easier to understand we have used the example of a mental health day centre and included a potential questionnaire. Throughout this chapter the reader will have observed how it is possible to involve service user co-researchers in the different aspects of the research process. The reader will have also noted that it cannot be assumed that all the training required for a research project can be completed up-front. In fact, issues surrounding data analysis and dissemination of the findings may only really come alive when the service user co-researchers have reached that part of the research process.

Summary

This chapter, and the previous one, have sought to identify a practical journey through the research cycle for service user co-researchers identifying key points, issues and practical examples of how the research process can be progressed successfully. As both chapters demonstrate, it is possible with a little imagination and training to be inclusive. There are limits as to the degree of service user co-researcher involvement. These limits are not so much derived form the status of being, or not being a service user, but the degree of training and skills of the service co-researchers. Many of these skills can be taught, but not every service user co-researcher will have the propensity to partake of the training or wish to do so. These practical chapters have demonstrated a number of levels of potential involvement, reminding us of our earlier discussion that to view service user involvement in research as a singular process is a misnomer. In reality it is more likely to be a profile with greater and lesser involvement depending on which part of the research process is being considered. The message, however, is clear; there is no reason why service user co-researchers cannot meaningfully be involved in research projects that would benefit from their service user experience.

Recommended reading

www.invo.org.uk/Database The INVOLVE website offers a database of service user involvement in research projects which can be searched by either stage of the research process or keyword

Leamy, M. and Clough, R. (2005) *Depending on Each Other: Teaching, Researching and Older People's Perspectives on Doing Research Together*, York: Joseph Rowntree Foundation.

Lowes, L. and Hulatt, I. (eds) (2005) *Involving Service Users in Health and Social Care Research*, Abingdon: Routledge. An edited collection providing a range of examples of service user involvement of different client groups in health and social care.

Nolan, M., Hanson, E., Grant, G. and Keady, J. (eds) (2007) *User Participation in Health and Social Care Research: Voices, Values and Evaluation*. Maidenhead: Open University Press. An edited collection of case studies of a range of service users' involvement in research.

Figure 6.1   Example Interview Schedule

Midtown Mental Health Outreach Services Study – For Service Users attending
Midtown Daycentre
Basic Details
Date.................
Start time of interview ....   *Finish Time....................*
Male/Female (Please circle one)
How would you describe your ethnic origin?
I am
White - British
White - Irish
Other White background
Black or Black British - Caribbean
Black or Black British - African
Other Black background
Asian or Asian British - Indian
Asian or Asian British - Pakistani
Asian or Asian British - Bangladeshi
Chinese or other Ethnic background - Chinese
Other Asian background
Mixed - White and Black Caribbean
Mixed - White and Black African
Mixed - White and Asian
Other Mixed background
Other Ethnic

What is your medical diagnosis?
..
Do you have a disability? YES/NO
If yes, what is the nature of your disability?
..
..

Who referred you to the outreach team?
Self referral   *GP*   *Community Mental Health Team*
Other – please specify ....

Questions about the respondent's attendance
(1) How long have you been attending the day centre?
less than 6 months   *up to 1 year*   *up to 2 years*   *up to 3 years*   *3 years +*
(Please circle one)
(2) How frequently do you attend?
Every day   *2–3 times per week*   *weekly*   *fortnightly*   *monthly*
Other (please specify)..
(3) How do you get to the day centre?
Walk   *car*   *bus*   *train*   *taxi*
Please circle the main method of transport
(4) Do you find it easy to travel to the day centre?
....
Why?
..
..

(5) Which sessions do you attend?
Drop-in   *Counselling*   *Job preparation*   *Healthy living*
Stress management   *Gardening*   *Research group*
(Please circle the ones attended)

Figure 6.1 *(Continued)*

(6) Which sessions do you value and why?

....
....
....
....

(7) If you were to attend for only one session, which one would it be?

....

(8) Why?

....
....
....

(9) Are there any other sessions you would like to attend? (if the respondent answers no to this question go straight to question 11)

....

(10) Why don't you attend these sessions?

....
....

(11) Are there any new sessions you would like to see included?

....
....

(12) What would you do if you did not attend the day centre?

....
....

Questions about the running of the centre
(13) Do you feel staff at the centre value you?

....
....

(14) Can you give me an example?

....
....

(15) How would you like to be treated by the staff?

....
....

(16) Can you get involved in the management of the centre? If yes, how?

....
....

(17) Do you feel that those attending the day centre are encouraged to contribute to the centre's management? Can you give me an example?

....
....

(18) If you had a magic wand and could make two wishes to improve the centre, what would they be?

....
....
....

(19) Is there anything you would like to tell me about the day centre I have not given you the opportunity to say?

....
....

Thank you for your time. Your answers will be treated in confidence; no names will be attached to the final report. Copies of the final report and an easy-to-read summary will be sent to the centre in May. Members of the research team will be attending a centre meeting after this date to discuss the report and its recommendations, please feel free to attend.

7 Involving Young Service Users in Health and Social Care Research

Introduction

Up until now we have explored service user involvement in research principally from an adult viewpoint. Traditionally, children's perspectives have been filtered through the interpretations of their parents, carers, teachers or researchers. This chapter seeks to highlight the key issues concerned in involving children as service user co-researchers. The first issue for us is what is a child? This has been a question of increasing interest in recent years in the work of Aries, who claimed that in the Western Europe of the Middle Ages children were seen as miniature adults. However, from about the 15th century onwards there is evidence of the emergence of a new category, childhood which was seen as distinct and different from adulthood (Rogers, 2001). This suggests that childhood is a social construction with no natural distinction that clearly defines children from other forms of intergenerational differentiation. It also needs to be acknowledged that our ideas about children are paradoxical. At one end of the spectrum we see children as innocents in need of adult care and protection; at the other end we view them as menacing and dangerous in need of control and incarceration. A paradox often played out in the media is with its images of needy children in charity adverts like those of the NSPCC and the demonization of those wearing hooded jackets – or 'hoodies' – and the current fears around the use of knives by teenagers. None of these fears are new, as Pearson (1983) observed in his book on hooliganism that looked at documentary evidence going back generation by generation. He identified that each generation had similar experiences of hooliganism even though each thought theirs was worse than the generation before and each thought they were experiencing the breakdown of civilized society.

It is quite clumsy to talk of children and young people as service user co-researchers throughout this chapter and, instead, the chapter, will use the phrase 'young service users' to capture those aged 0–18 years, in line with our current child care legislation in the UK and the United Nations Convention on the Rights of the Child. This is patently not to suggest that the needs of a 3-year-old are the same as a 16-year-old or that you should necessarily treat them the same. The importance of age will be discussed, but the convention of younger service user co-researcher will be used for the ease of the reader.

Some of the differences between the approach with adults and that of involving younger service user co-researchers are differences of degree; others are differences of kind. In this chapter we will highlight both kinds of differences. It must also be remembered that children and young people are not a homogeneous group, they may also have physical disabilities, mental health difficulties, be unaccompanied asylum seekers, be in foster homes or have been the subject of a child safeguarding case conference. This is not to forget that there may be other differences due to gender, ethnic grouping, sexuality, social class, whether they live in urban or rural settings, social class and so on. Children and young people, like adults, are a complex heterogeneous grouping artificially bounded for the ease of academic discussion.

Reflexive Questions

＊ What do you think are the key differences between involving young service users in research as opposed to involving adults? What impact do you think these differences make on the way research can be conducted and the roles that young researchers can undertake?

In particular, this chapter highlights the mandate for involving young service users and the importance of recent understandings about childhood. The chapter also reviews the costs and benefits of involving young service users as co-researchers, practical and ethical concerns, issues related to the legal position of young people, and safeguarding young service users.

The mandate for involvement

Before identifying the differences, it is important to remind ourselves that there is a mandate for the involvement of children and young people in the services they receive. This comes both from international and national perspectives. Internationally the United Nations *Convention on the Rights of the Child* (United Nations, 1989) is very significant as it established the standard for the rights of children everywhere. It should, however, be noted that the UK government has not adopted it as part of its legislative framework, whilst the US and Somalia are not signatories (Johns, 2003). Those countries which are signatories are inspected at least once in every five years to establish how their child care and legal systems are meeting the requirements of the convention. Of particular interest to us are Articles 12 and 13. Article 12 promotes a child's or young person's right to express their views and for these views to be heard in any matter or procedure affecting them. These views must also be given due weight in concurrence with the age and maturity of the child. Article 13 promotes the right to information and freedom of expression through any medium of the child or young person's choice. It is quite clear that health and social care services which impact upon children and young people would come under both these articles. In Denmark the educational regulations explicitly require schools to develop children's skills in learning to participate in decision-making (Taylor, 2000).

In a UK perspective there has been a duty to consult children and young people since the 1975 Children Act (Freeman et al., 1996). The involvement of children and young people has also been part of the modernization thesis of the New Labour administrations under Tony Blair, with the government's position clearly stated by the Children and Young People's Unit:

> The government wants children and young people to have more opportunities to get involved in the design and evaluation of services that affect them or which they might use. (Children and Young People's Unit, 2001: 2)

This has since been reinforced by the *National Service Framework for Children, Young People and Maternity Services* (Department of Health and Department for Education and Skills, 2004). There has also been the establishment of a children's commissioner in each of the four UK nations. It is thus possible to suggest that the promotion of empowerment and involvement of children and young people should also transfer to research. It does not make sense that this level of involvement should only be restricted to educational, social or health related activities. It also needs to transfer to other aspects of children and young people's lives. Thus it is suggested that the involvement of young service users as co-researchers is not merely a research agenda but also a participation agenda (Roberts, 2004).

The mandate for the involvement of young service users as co-researchers shares many similarities of that with adults. There is, though, an imperative with children and young people in that, if they can experience meaningful involvement as children and young people, this is likely to transfer as an expectation to later life and potentially strengthens our democracy.

Children and young people's participation

In recent years there has been a change from our Victorian assumption that 'children should be seen but not heard'. As identified in Chapter 1 it is possible to see children and young people as objects, subjects, social actors or active participants. The first perspective treats children and young people as objects to be acted on and researched. The second perspective is an improvement on the first position as it brings children and young people to the foreground of research and promotes a move towards a more child and young person centred approach. However, this approach remains tempered by the view of adults as to the ability and maturity of young people (Robinson and Kellet, 2004). Christensen and Prout's (2002) third perspectives sees children and young people as social actors who are authors of their own lives and who are both able to change and be changed by acting in the world. The fourth perspective is a special case of this where children and young people are seen as active participants in the research process and act as co-researchers. Traditionally, research has been 'on' children and then moved to being 'with' children, and more recently to more empowering approaches 'to' children (Borland et al., 2001). Christensen and James (2000) argue that there is a need for a mind shift in researching children whereby researchers consider both their ethical and practical responsibility to ensure that children's marginalized position in relation to adults is considered throughout their research. At this point it is useful to review what are the benefits and costs of involving children and young people in research as co-researchers.

Benefits and costs

> **Reflexive Questions**
>
> ❋ Before beginning to identify the benefits and costs for involving children and young people in research, can you identify what you see as the benefits and costs for the research, the co-researchers and adult researchers researcher? Are these different from what you would consider as the benefits and costs for adult patients or service users in a similar study?

❖ *Benefits*

Similar to adult co-researchers (Smith et al., 2002; Jones, 2004; Kirby, 2004; McLaughlin, 2005) state that children and young people:

- can identify research issues and questions overlooked by adult researchers;
- enhance the range and quality of data collected;
- speak a common language not always accessible to adults;
- can help ensure that the research tools, e.g. questionnaires, interview schedules, consent forms, information leaflets use understandable language;

- can help with the recruitment of peers as co-researchers or service users;
- gain access to places where adults would not be welcome;
- advise on the user-friendliness of any publication and alternative formats like webpages, CDs or podcasts;
- can help disseminate results.

It could be claimed that we have all been children and therefore you do not need young service users as co-researchers as adults could be seen as 'proxy children'. This would be a mistake, as Save the Children (2004: 13) observed: 'Adult researchers may have less insight into the daily lives of children than they think they have'. It is also worthwhile remembering that young people may view other young people as more expert than adults in certain issues. Butler et al. (2002) identified that in divorce cases young people will often turn to their friends who have had a similar experience to find out what their parents' divorce is likely to mean for them rather than to adults.

On a different level the very involvement of young service users as co-researchers can lead organizations to challenge their traditional ways of working. The involvement of children and young people in research can begin to change the balance of power and promote the view of children and young people as co-creators of knowledge (Godfrey, 2005).

There are thus a lot of benefits for research and development in involving young service users as co-researchers. There are also identifiable benefits for the co-researchers. As co-researchers they can actively participate in developing answers to the issues that affect their own lives and those of their peers. Being involved in research can improve confidence, improve self-esteem and improve employability by developing new marketable skills. This can also promote active citizenship and reduce exclusion where children and young people's co-researchers are being listened to and where they can see that their views matter.

Benefits are not merely restricted to the research and co-researchers but also to the adult researchers. Being involved with a group of young co-researchers provides an opportunity for the adult researcher to increase their knowledge and understanding of children and youth issues. It will also potentially lead to a deeper awareness of children and young people's concerns, which can only benefit the adult researcher who is sensitively seeking to research the child and young person's world. Practically, it is also likely to be helpful when considering recommendations for the development of services to consider these from the perspectives and needs of the children and young people rather than double guessing what children and young people want. One benefit not written about in the textbooks is that working with children and young people can be great fun (McLaughlin, 2005).

Clearly, there are identifiable benefits for research in involving young service users as co-researchers. However, as Kirby (2004) points out, these benefits do not necessarily translate into a better research project.

❖ Costs

Involving young service users as co-researchers can be costly both in terms of time and resources.

> All participatory research projects (whether this is with older adults or young people) need the time and resources to support participation. This is easy to underestimate. Time is needed to contact and recruit young people, and to support them in contributing at different stages of the research. Support workers are likely to be needed to work with the young people. (Kirby, 2004: 12)

Involving service users in research is resource intensive and to involve young service users as co-researchers is likely to be even more resource intensive. Prior to recruitment adult researchers should have a Criminal Records Bureau (CRB) check to satisfy the research commissioner that they have no convictions that would present a risk to working with children. If the research is working with young people as co-researchers who are beyond the age of compulsory schooling the research commissioner and adult researcher may also need to ensure that these young people are similarly CRB checked. An acceptable CRB check may need to be added to the person specification of a young person's co-researchers. Sending off, paying for and awaiting the return of CRB checks takes both time and resources.

Once a group of children or young people's co-researchers are identified they will require a support worker. Such workers can act as taxi-drivers, facilitators, problem solvers, mentors and general 'dogsbody'. Support workers help to ensure that children and young people are able to attend any meetings, training or research sites, are safe whilst undertaking research and are kept informed of what is happening and why (McLaughlin, 2004). This requires the lead researcher to be able to work with both the support workers and the co-researchers, bringing an extra layer of complexity into an already complex situation.

Unlike adults, depending on the age of the children or young people, the adult researcher may not only need to secure the carer's consent that they engage in the research but will also have to get their school's agreement if they are of statutory school age. Neither of these is necessarily straightforward. Carers may not wish to give their permission but their child or young person may wish to take part. Or, the carers may wish their son or daughter to take part but the son or daughter does not; or even more problematic, when the carer encourages their son or daughter to take part so that they can know what is happening in the research. Carers need to be made aware that what any co-researcher finds out in the research is confidential, which means that they need to resist their natural urges to finding out the details of the research. This can be difficult for carers to accept, especially if the research is likely to raise painful or sensitive issues. Cree et al. (2002) also found that this was the case where the subject is potentially stigmatizing for the parents such as studies in relation to the impact of parental mental ill health or HIV/Aids.

When considering the recruitment of young service user co-researchers there is also a need to consider if the children or young people are subject to any legal orders. If the child or young person is the subject of a Care Order the adult researcher will also need to request permission form the local authority for the child or young person to be able to take part in the research.

In all of this it is easy to forget that young co-researchers need to give their 'consent' to be involved in a research project. In research involving children there is an important distinction between the concepts of consent and assent. Consent implies permission from someone who has legal authority such as a parent, guardian or local authority, whilst assent signifies voluntary agreement from someone without legal authority. For young people who are 'Gillick competent' (see discussion later in this chapter) it can be assumed they are sufficiently able to give their own permission. Although, as Lamprill (2002: 2) observes, it would be a 'foolhardy investigator who consented a child into a trial against parental wishes'. Thus, for most young co-researchers the best that can be hoped for is their assent to take part after they have been fully advised of what they are being asked to do, what training will be offered, what risks are likely and what rewards they will receive.

Whilst the adult co-researcher may have to structure their involvement in any research alongside their work or other commitments, children and young people are in a different structural position and relationship with their education. Whereas many schools are very happy to encourage such involvement in research, service user co-researchers of statutory school age have to notify their local education welfare department, who have the right to refuse their consent. Failure to obtain such agreement may invalidate the research's insurance policy. Any research strategy is further complicated as it has to be negotiated around school terms, exams and school holidays and employment legislation for school children – which will be discussed later.

Working with children and young people also highlights the problematic issue of 'peerness'. Jones (2004) found that some peer researchers had such similar experiences to the young interviewers that they had difficulty in separating out the research answers from their own issues. This is not to say that it could not be done, but that the training process will need to develop skills in this area. For children and young people who become service users co-researchers are chosen because of their experiences of health and social care, but it is important that this familiarity with the issues does not lead to the silencing of other voices.

'Peerness' also raises other issues. Can you assume that an 18-year-old is a peer of an 8-year-old although both may be black, in foster care or suffering from leukaemia? Whilst we might agree that the age difference here is too great, what about a 13-year-old and a 16-year-old? Or does it matter if the age is the same but both come from different ethnic origins? It is not the intention to give an exact definition of 'peerness' but to raise an issue that does not appear to be so critical in working with adult service users. Children and young people have a greater sensitivity to age possibly because their lives and progress are aligned at school or youth club by the age they are. UK society demonstrates its ambiguity towards young people by saying young people are culpable for criminal offences from the age of 10, are assessed as an adult at 14 in order to buy a bus ticket, are allowed to marry with their parents' permission at 16, drive a motor vehicle at 17 but are only able to vote when they are 18.

Whilst the similarity in age of service user co-researchers and service respondents is often seen as a positive benefit of this approach, aspects such as gender (McLaughlin, 2004) and local accent (McCartan et al., 2004) can also have an impact. Gender can be an important consideration, especially when teenage girls are interviewing teenage boys who may feel it is more an opportunity to find a girlfriend than to answer the questions. This is not to say that we should just have same sex interviews, but it is a subject that does need to be considered. Similarly, there is some evidence that local accent can have a detrimental impact on the quality of the research data. Issues like sexuality, disability and ethnicity are likely to pose similar issues.

Young people's lives are bounded and move to a different rhythm than those of adults. Issues like friends, partners, sports, youth clubs, school and or music can take precedence over the research process. Adult researchers also need to consider over-recruiting the number of young service users required, as all these activities, and more, may make it difficult to retain young service users' involvement. It is not, for example, unusual for two young people as boyfriend and girlfriend to join a project and for one to leave when their relationship breaks up. Similarly, Wadham and Storey (2004) expressed frustration at a young service user's reference group, who invited them to a meeting at short notice only to find the membership had totally changed, requiring them to go over the information they had presented before.

Having considered some of the costs from the perspective of the research process, it is also important to look at these from the perspective of the young co-researchers and the adult researcher.

The most important cost to the young co-researchers is time, in particular, the opportunity cost that is part of being involved as a member of a research team. If young co-researchers were not involved in research they could be engaging in leisure activities, playing with friends, 'hanging about', finding boyfriends or girlfriends, studying or earning money.

There is also a risk that children and young people who come forward as potential co-researchers will have their inadequacies exposed at the expense of their strengths if the process is not inclusive or takes account of the abilities and maturity of the co-researchers. Young co-researchers cannot be assumed to have the same knowledge or experience base as research assistants. They also cannot be assumed to learn in the same way as adults, and training programmes need to be demystifying, fun, problem-based, practical, activity oriented and pedagogically aware of how children and young people learn. This is not to say that adults will not learn in similar ways, but it will require adult researchers to develop new skills.

For adult researchers the involvement of young co-researchers in collaborative research costs time, energy and resources (McLaughlin, 2006; Swallow et al., 2007). Working with young service users is likely to mean that the research will take longer due to the recruitment, training, the extra legal and ethical issues that need to be considered, the support of the support workers, the need to go at the young service user co-researcher's pace whilst not forgetting the different rhythm of children and young person's lives. Navigating the way through research ethic committees can be difficult in collaborative research at the best of times but introducing young co-researchers to the equation can make this process even more difficult. Local authorities are still coming to terms with the Research Governance Framework (DH, 2001a; DH et al., 2008) and many children's services have yet to come on board. There are also concerns about the NHS Research Ethics Committees, who are seen as unsympathetic to collaborative approaches in general and to research involving young service users in particular (Lewis, 2002; Godfrey, 2004).

It is important to ensure that the co-researchers are not exploited in the process and adult researchers will need to ensure costs are built in for expenses and travel. There are also the financial costs of the support workers and the costs for providing support to both the research respondents and young co-researchers in their interviews if they should trigger painful memories or experiences.

Working with young service users is not for every researcher. It will require high energy levels, the ability to expect the unexpected and the need to develop both research project management skills and skills in youth work and community development. Young service users can be very enthusiastic and committed and this is likely to tax the personal skills of the researcher.

> **Practice Examples**
>
> *In working with young service users as co-researchers the author has experienced the following examples of expecting the unexpected and the need for a wider skills set:*
>
> (a) *On taking a group of young people away for training aged between 16 and 21 it was agreed that they would not consume alcohol at the bar at our accommodation. Unbeknown to the author, there was a 24-hour Tesco supermarket behind the accommodation and the older young people, who felt their natural rights had been infringed, went to the supermarket and obtained alcohol for the whole group. At 3.00 am in the morning one of the young co-researchers discovered how to use the internal phone and started ringing everyone.*
>
> (b) *On travelling to a research site the author found himself stuck at Euston with a 17-year-old girl and without an onward train to the South Coast. It could have been possible to have secured a hotel room for the evening but I don't think that would have gone down particularly well with the funder or the University. It was decided to get a taxi which broke down once we got outside London!!!*
>
> (c) *On a research project working with two different geographically areas it was decided to undertake the first set of interviews together and arrange to visit a research site at half-term. It was only later discovered that the two different areas had different half-terms.*

In working with young service user co-researchers there is a limit to the types of research that can be undertaken. Although adult service users may have both the personal and academic skills, it is unlikely that young service users will have the necessary academic skills, even if they do have effective personal communication skills. As previously noted, it may be difficult to identify research that could not be added to from the point of young co-researchers; this is, however, different from saying young co-researchers will have the abilities to undertake advanced level research activities. This means that there will be a limit to the different types of research that can be undertaken.

Lastly, there is a cost also identified with adult service users. Adult researchers seeking to build, or maintain, a research career need to be seen to be publishing, and in particular in internationally peer reviewed journal articles, the current standard by which research output is generally measured. This can be difficult in projects which take greater amounts of time, and time taken in preparation to work with young service user co-researchers is time that cannot be spent writing.

Given the benefits and costs of involving young service users as co-researchers, it is clear that there is an impelling case for this involvement, but the fact that it does contain risks and costs should not be underestimated.

The research cycle

Before looking at the research cycle it should be acknowledged that, although there are not lots of examples of young service user controlled research, it is not impossible that these will not develop in the future. In consequence, what is considered below is within the notion of collaborative research whereby the young service user co-researchers' views are sought, taken seriously and then it is possible to identify where their contributions have impacted upon and changed the research for better or for worse. The involvement of young co-researchers is not seen as 'window dressing' or being 'politically correct' but represents an authentic attempt to undertake research within a collaborative approach to make a genuine contribution to knowledge.

Keeping in line with the two previous chapters, it is worthwhile considering the research cycle and the implications of this for how the young service user co-researcher can contribute. Many of the issues are the same, but different, and this section will highlight some of these differences.

It is not impossible for young service users to be involved in the conception of a research project although it still remains unlikely. It is also probable that even if a research project is identified by children and young people they will require adult help in putting their ideas into an acceptable form for research commissioners. Currently, the involvement of young service users in research is more likely to have been an adult decision than a child's or young person's. This immediately raises a challenge for all those adults working with young co-researchers, who need to ensure that adult involvement in the process does not become adult management and thus undermines the young service user's co-researcher's ownership of the research project. Adult workers have to be continually on their guard to avoid adult-filtered intervention undermining authentic young service user co-research (Kellett, 2005).

Once the recruitment of potential service user co-researchers has been undertaken a training programme will need to be established which can be differentiated by age and ability of the group. This programme will need to be engaging for the young co-researchers whilst at the same time covering the necessary academic and practical skills input. Just because you are working with young service user co-researchers there is no reason why the training should not be undertaken in an intellectually honest manner. The use of interactive games and activities can be successfully used to convey the content. Clark (2006) describes a mosaic approach for meaningfully involving young children in research whilst Cocks (2006) identifies research strategies for engaging children with learning disabilities. Tarleton et al. (2004) have written that the experience of research of children with learning disabilities has been to be measured, quantified and pathologized. In contrast they describe how young people with learning difficulties can be involved in research steering groups and make a valuable contribution to the conduct of the research. This is to suggest that there is no 'natural' reason why certain groups of children and young people should not be involved as co-researchers. There will be limits to their involvement, but these limits often say more about our abilities to be innovative and to think 'outside of the box'.

In a similar vein it should not be assumed that young service users can only interview other young people and cannot interview staff. Whilst McLaughlin (2005) reports positively on this happening, Kirby (1999) cautions that both the young co-researchers and adults may feel intimidated by the reversal of power relations. Kirby goes on to describe a project by West (1997), in which the local authority refused to let the peer researchers, who had previously been in care, interview care workers for a study on young care leavers' needs. What this highlights is the need to prepare both the young co-researchers and adults for the research experience. Because something is difficult it is not the same as saying that it is inappropriate or unhelpful. There will be circumstances when adults may decide that it is too sensitive for young service users to interview their service providers, but this should not be seen as the norm as it potentially devalues what young service user co-researchers can contribute to our knowledge of service provision.

Reflexive Questions

* How do you think a young service user co-researcher should deal with a research respondent who said they had been sexually abused? Would you choose the same position if this was a 10-year-old or a 17-year-old? Would this change if either has a younger sibling at home?

It is important to consider how service user co-researchers will deal with confidentiality issues such as mental health, cancer, domestic violence, child sexual abuse or criminal behaviour should these be disclosed within an interview. Strategies for dealing with such disclosures need to be considered as part of the training programme and revisited during the research phase to ensure that the young co-researchers feel confident about how to handle these should they arise. Research confidentiality usually entails taking care not to pass on information in any way to those concerned with the research respondent, or disclosing information only in ways in which the respondent could not be identified. There are ethical considerations with children that mean that these normal assurances cannot be given.

> There are two areas of particular concern: where a child discloses he or she is being seriously harmed or ill treated, and where the researcher identifies a condition, for example a medical condition or learning difficulty about which the parents could take action. Failure of the researcher to take appropriate action might not only lead to criticism on ethical grounds, but in some limited circumstances it could also give rise to legal liability. (Masson, 2004: 52)

Dealing with such research respondent disclosures is not straightforward. For instance, what do you do if a 10-year-old child tells you that they are being sexually abused but do not want you to tell anyone else about it? You will not be able to agree to their request for confidentiality due to their age and vulnerability. Whilst if a 17-year-old was to say the same thing, their request for confidentiality might be respected, although further questions may need to be asked by the young co-researcher (depending on age and maturity), or by an adult researcher, to ensure that there are no other children at risk in the household. In these circumstances it is neither the adult's nor the young service user co-researcher's duty to probe further or to investigate. Researchers should listen carefully, recording any information and being aware that any conversation may later be used as testimony in a court setting (Masson, 2005). Adult researchers also need to be aware of local child safeguarding procedures so that a referral for investigation, if required, can be made quickly. It is best if issues on confidentiality or when to 'breach trust' can be included in the information for research respondents so that they are aware of any limitations to the confidentiality principle.

Deciding upon what age or the degree of maturity that is required to accede to request for information to be treated as confidential is not straightforward. Following the 1985 'Gillick' decision in the courts by Lord Scarman, the right to consent and confidentiality was given to under 16-year-olds who requested contraceptive advice. This has been widened out to become known as 'Gillick competency' referring to those under 16 who can be seen to have sufficient knowledge and understanding to give their own consent, and that a parent does not have the right to override that consent (Thurston and Church, 2001). Such consent is not based purely on age, as Alderson and Montgomery (1996) argued that children with chronic health conditions such as cystic fibrosis are often well versed in the nature of their condition following in-depth discussions with medical staff. Thurston and Church (2001: 228) thus identify that: 'relevant experience of illness, treatment or disability is far more salient than age for acquiring competence'.

This awareness can be transferred to the research situation, but will not prevent the need for any research situation to be considered individually. Both ethical and criminal considerations will need to be thought about in response to the duty of care and the need to prevent further criminal activity. This can especially be difficult for research respondents when they are deemed to be 'Gillick competent' but the risk to a sibling in the same household is assessed as too great to leave the matter unreported. In these circumstances it is important to make sure the respondent is aware of what you are doing, why you are doing it and if there is anything else you can help them with or refer them to.

The second aspect of the Masson (2004) quotation above considered the situation where the researcher identifies a medical condition or learning difficulty about which the parents, or carers, could have taken action but have not done so. Whilst this is possible, it is unlikely. Young service user co-researchers will identify such situations However, this will be another subject that will need to be considered during training and once the research is underway.

Prior to the research beginning it is also important to clarify how the young service user co-researchers will be rewarded and recognized for their contributions. As Hill (2005) observes there are different views as to whether children and young people should be paid or not. For some the mere idea of paying young people is tantamount to bribery, whilst for others it is the logical recompense for their time and effort. The idea of paying young service user co-researchers and research respondents can create difficulties for research commissioners who fear that any money will be used to pay for drugs, cigarettes or alcohol. This often results in young co-researchers being given vouchers. However, this paternalistic view may give research commissioners a false sense of comfort, as who is say that either the young people would not sell the voucher, or use it for other necessary items and use the cash saved to spend in less acceptable ways. There is also an issue that the young service user co-researchers are deemed competent to manage the research relationship but not manage money. One last consideration for adult researchers is that they must be mindful of parents' wishes for younger children and that paying young service user co-researchers may have a negative impact on a family's entitlement to state benefits (Jones, 2004).

Alongside this issue of whether young co-researchers are rewarded with money or vouchers is the acknowledgement that young people are treated differently to adults in employment law. Although there is a minimum wage and it is legal to pay young people less it is questionable whether it is ethically just to pay young service user co-researchers less than their adult counterparts for the same activity. Young service user co-researchers are thus more open to financial exploitation than adult service user co-researchers. There are also major limitations on the employment of young people under the age of 16 years throughout the UK. Those below 14 years old generally may not be employed. This means that young service user co-researchers are likely to be legally considered as sessional workers rather than employees. Whilst it may be legal to consider young service user co-researchers in this way it is certainly not ethical. Given the vulnerability of children and young people they need to be treated to the highest employment standards not the lowest. There are also health and safety requirements on under 18s which require employers to assess the risks posed by the work, taking account of, among other things, the immaturity and inexperience of the young people (Masson, 2004).

One other area worthy of mention here includes young co-researchers' potential exposure to discriminatory attitudes and behaviours in relation to racism, homophobia, ageism, xenophobia, disablism and other forms of abuse. Training for young service user co-researchers will need to consider how these issues can be managed, including when it is appropriate to end an interview and who to pass such comments onto. Young co-researchers should not be left to deal with such abuses by themselves.

We have already alluded to the need for young service users to retain confidentiality about anything they may hear or read, and Smith et al. (2002) have identified particular difficulties with this. There is a natural tendency to wish to share with friends and families the interesting things we do, and being involved in research as a young co-researcher, we hope, would be one of the more interesting things. There is thus a need to remind young service users of their ethical responsibilities and in certain cases it may lead to individual children or young people being asked to leave the project. Coyne (1998) also notes carers may wish to know what young co-researchers have been up to and, in certain cases, this may either require the adult researcher to speak to the carer to advise them that this is not ethical, or that the young co-researcher will need to be withdrawn from the research team.

Young service user co-researchers can be involved in both the data collection and data analysis where appropriate training has been given to help them contribute effectively. As mentioned previously, with proper preparation and training young service user co-researchers can interview service providers. This may also be an indicator of how child friendly services are by the response they give the young co-researchers. Put another way, health and social care teams who provide services for children and young people would claim to treat children and young people with respect and here is an opportunity to witness this in action. This will be especially the case in those governmental and voluntary organizations who explicitly state that part of their remit is to empower children and young people: in these cases it would seem strange if the staff were not part of the study.

It has often proven difficult for researchers to get young people involved in the writing up of research (McLaughlin, 2005). This has resulted in the completion of final reports taking much longer than first planned. However, this may be about the nature of being a service user under certain conditions. Thus, we know that young care leavers are severely disadvantaged in relation to their educational attainment in comparison with children and young people living with their parents. In 2006 43 per cent of young people leaving care had one GSCE or GNVQ whilst only 7 per cent had five GCSEs at A–C grade which is the level for considering A levels and moving onto higher education (www.dfes.gov.uk/rgateway/DB/SFK/s000691/SF44-2006.pdf accessed 29 November 2007). This is compared to 98 per cent and 62 per cent respectively for the population as a whole over the same period (http:/news.bbc.co.uk/1/hi/education/5278774.stm accessed 27th November 2007).

This is not necessarily because of the experience of care but may also be due to the conditions surrounding an initial admission to care which is likely to have included a disrupted educational attendance and performance. The request for young service user co-researchers to write may link to difficulties with writing at school, or feel like they are being asked to complete homework and may thus be less attractive for some children and young people. Adult researchers should also look at other ways in which young service user co-researchers can contribute to the final report, which may include drawings, poetry, photography or short reflective comments at the end of each chapter.

This again raises the issue of whether full names, nicknames or pseudonyms are used in a final report and who has the right to say which is used. Punch (1998) records how research respondents may feel embarrassed or upset by research results and this would also be a potential risk for young service user co-researchers. If they happen to be dealing with sensitive areas like teenage pregnancy, sexually transmitted diseases, drug misuse, child abuse or the experience of young people living with domestic violence, then to be named as service user co-researcher would be to indicate to the outside world that they are teenage parents, have a sexually transmitted disease, use drugs, suffered child abuse or had lived in a domestic violence household. A judgement needs to be made before any final publication which raises the ethical challenge of 'Gillick competency', the role of carers in the decision-making process and the importance of the morally active researcher. It is quite likely that carers would not want to draw attention to their children and young people's anti-social behaviours, even if the young service user co-researchers wanted their names on the research report. In settling this potential conflict, adult researchers need to undertake a risk assessment and discharge their duty of care to ensure that no young service user co-researcher is worse off at the end of the research than they were at the beginning.

Young service users have proved very capable of bringing research alive and disseminating results at conferences or paper interviews (Kirby, 2004). It is, however, important again to ensure they are properly prepared for such experiences: it cannot be assumed they will naturally have the ability to speak in front of audiences.

Lastly, it is important to consider how to end the research. Children and younger people will have invested a lot in the research process and it is a responsibility of the adult researcher that this is marked in a way that signals the end of the process, celebrates the successes of the research and acknowledges a change in the adult service user co-researcher relationship. Young co-researchers will often have ideas how this can best be managed. It is also unlikely, as opposed to some adult service user researchers, that the children and young people will develop a young service user research career. Partly, this is because they will not remain children and young people indefinitely and that there are fewer external opportunities for children and young people to become involved in research.

At the start of this chapter you were asked to consider the benefits and costs of involving young service user co-researchers as opposed to adult service user co-researchers. This chapter has sought to demonstrate that there are close similarities and differences of degree and kind. The major benefits to research are similar to both groups including helping to focus research, ensuring the languages of interviews or questionnaires are user friendly, data collection and analysis and dissemination of results. The areas where differences appear include the issues to do with recruitment and the need to gain the permission of carers, schools and the local authority for children on care orders to gain access to young service user co-researchers. These legal requirements are also mirrored in employment legislation and the amounts of time young people are allowed to work. This situation is further complicated with the 'Gillick competency' and being able to decide when young people are able to make decisions without reference to their carers. Similarly there is a major difference in issues to do with confidentiality as the research respondents, like the co-researchers, are children and young people, and issues of child safeguarding need to be to the forefront of the research. Issues, which are more of degree than kind, include matters like: training, reward and recognition, need for support workers, data collection, data analysis, authorship and endings. This is not to suggest that adult researchers can work collaboratively with both groups; in fact the opposite may be true – some researchers may only work best with adults and others only work best with children.

Summary

This chapter has traced the involvement of children and young people as service user co-researchers. The chapter has looked at these issues both from the perspective of costs and benefits and the research cycle. From all of this it was clear that whilst there are many similarities to research with adult service users there are also some significant differences associated with children's age and maturity, legal status, power, education and limitations of confidentiality. Developments in our understanding of involving young service user co-researchers go both hand-in-hand with the developments for adults, but also, separately in relation to the structural position that children hold within Western society. This chapter challenges us to be creative and innovative in the way we involve children and young people as, without their perspectives, there cannot be a full understanding of paediatric care, child safeguarding services, residential care or education.

> Knowledge about children is incomplete unless it takes into account the knowledge that children have of themselves. (Jones, 2004: 114)

Recommended reading

Fraser, S., Lewis, V., Ding, S., Kellett, M. and Robinson, C. *Doing Research with Children and Young People*, London: Sage in association with the Open University. This is an edited collection of chapters providing a good oversight of the key issues in involving children and young people in research.

Kirby, P. (2004) *A Guide to Actively Involving Young People in Research: Fore Researchers, Research Commissioners and Managers*, Eastleigh: Involve. This is an easy-to-read guide identifying the benefits and how to involve young people in research. This publication can also be downloaded from the Involve website www.invo.org.uk.

McLaughlin, H. (2006) 'Involving young service users as co-researchers: Possibilities, benefits and costs', *British Journal of Social Work*, 36 (8): 1395–1410. This article provides an evaluation of the costs and benefits of involving young service user co-researchers.

Save the Children (2004) *So You Want to Involve Children in Research: A Toolkit for Supporting Children's Meaningful and Ethical Participation in Research Relating to Violence Against Children*. Stockholm: Save the Children. This can also be downloaded at: www.savethechildren.net/alliance/resources/So_you_want_to_research_apr2004pdf. This publication provides practical tips, ideas and guidance about how to involve young people as researchers.

Futures Imperfect

Introduction

In this the final chapter it is intended to review the implications of our previous discussions on the development of service user involvement in research. Following this analysis we look towards potential futures for involving service users in research in health and social care. This book has been an invitation to a debate and discussion that seeks to challenge current conceptions of how service users may be involved in research. It is accepted that this is a contested and contestable subject that vacillates between those who see it as a passing fad and those who see it as the only 'authentic' form of research. For some it occupies a 'morally impervious position' that is increasingly 'resistant to criticism' (Hodgson and Canvin, 2005). It is hoped that this book has not given that impression, but rather it has tried to tread a path that is aware of both the strengths and weakness of such approaches whilst also acting as a stimulus and springboard for others to begin to untangle the complex issues for themselves.

Reflexive Questions

❋ Before the key themes are reviewed you might like to put down three bullet points of what you consider to be your most important learning points from reading this book. You also might like to write down three questions about what you would like to find further answers about so that you could understand this area of study more fully.

Development of service user involvement in research in health and social care

Chapter 1 was primarily concerned with setting the context for involvement in research in health and social care. This chapter sought to get behind some of the taken-for-granted assumptions and identify the context in which service user involvement has developed. Managerial and democratic drivers were identified as key to the promotion of service user involvement in research. It was acknowledged that it was an increasingly common practice today to talk of 'health and social care' as if they were the same thing. Certainly this has been the direction of travel during the Blair and Thatcher governments with no sign of a change in the current administration. Professionals continue to be viewed as part of the problem as opposed to part of the solution. Service users want services that match their needs not what professionals deign they should have. If someone required a district nurse, aids to support daily living, bereavement counselling, a home help and advice about their benefits, they were less concerned about who provided these services than that the services were provided. It did not matter whether they were health or social care workers as long as the services were delivered. To this end to view health and social care as a single entity is understandable from a service user perspective. However, when we examined these concepts further we identified notable differences: health services are universalistic, social care is not; health services are free at the point of delivery, social care is not, whilst it was acknowledged that both services have developed their own cultures of practice. Differences like these are fundamental to the operation of these services and it is not hard to see why joint teams have found it difficult to work together.

We also deconstructed how we described the relationship between the professionals and those who they are paid to work with. In particular, we examined the assumptions behind the notions of: patient, client, consumer or customer, service user or expert by experience. All these terms were found to be wanting. In fact it was not possible to identify a satisfactory term that sought to equalize the power imbalance in the relationship. Whilst service user is the term most commonly used at present, it is suggested that in less than five years it will have gone out of fashion. All this highlighted that the involvement of service users in social policy and research is still a relatively new, often confusing but exciting area of development.

Why service users bother

In trying to understand the importance of service users to research we examined the motivation of those who became involved in research. In particular we highlighted that service users' experience of services has led many to seek to become involved in research to improve the situation for future service users. We then acknowledged and examined the benefits and costs for research and development, service user co-researchers and academic researchers in involving service users as co-researchers. From this it was clear there were tangible benefits for involvement but that these needed to be weighed against the costs. Involving service users as co-researchers is not cost neutral and should not be entered into lightly.

A simple four-stage model of involvement was identified: tokenism, consultation, collaboration and service user controlled research. It was argued that it was important to maintain tokenism as a point on the continuum as there were many examples of tokenism masquerading as involvement. Consultation was viewed as a concept open to wide interpretation and with meaningful involvement only really beginning at the collaborative and service user controlled ends of the continuum. The reader was also cautioned against viewing research and this continuum as a linear process and instead encouraged to consider it as an involvement profile where you needed to consider the degree of service user co-researcher involvement desired and attainable at each point in the research cycle. Service user controlled research was also shown to be an exciting, if somewhat contested internally and externally, development in service user involvement in research.

Ethical issues in involving service users as co-researchers

Chapter 3 examined the often overlooked area of ethics and service user involvement in research. Following an analysis of the development of research codes it was noted that acting ethically was more than merely implementing a research code. To act ethically requires the lead researcher to develop, in conjunction with the service user co-researchers, the attitude of a morally active researcher. There then followed a detailed analysis of the ethical issues to be considered at each state of the research process, acknowledging that whilst many ethical issues can be identified for the research governance process many others will only come to light once the research is underway. Key issues considered included the importance of questioning who funds research, informing-for-consent, anonymity and confidentiality, reward and recognition, support for service user co-researchers, authorship, dissemination and endings. From this chapter it is clear that there are significant ethical challenges that need to be considered in involving service users as co-researchers which go beyond that of a normal research project. It is also important to remember that it is contradictory to talk of an empowering participatory research approach if the research is undertaken in an unethical manner.

Philosophical issues in involving service users in research

In this chapter we identified the importance of ontology, epistemology and methodology, showing how each is related but can be viewed from very different perspectives. We noted that traditional realism and idealism now have a number of revisions seeking to bridge the differences between these two extremes. Similarly, we looked at the positivist and constructivist epistemological claims, noting how these all suggested incommensurable positions; to believe in a positivist position is to deny the possibility of a constructivist position and vice versa. When this was translated to methodologies it was seen that this was an untenable position as it is quite common to see studies which employ mixed methods, mixing both qualitative and quantitative methods together.

In translating this to the philosophical knowledge claims made for service user involvement in research, there was an identified bias towards qualitative approaches but the service user researcher also needs to be conversant in quantitative methods. Whilst we supported the development of advocacy/participatory claims to knowledge we critically examined and found wanting standpoint epistemology, which privileged service user knowledge at the expense of all other knowledge claims. For service user involvement in research to be meaningful it must meet the same general canons of knowledge claiming as other types of research. This should not be seen as a burden for service user involvement in research but a standard that is both attainable and desirable. From this chapter it was claimed that there is no reason why research involving service users as co-researchers should be denied claims to knowledge although these claims need to be tempered by the nature of the research undertaken, its philosophical underpinnings and the methods chosen.

Practical issues in involving service users in research

Chapters 6 and 7 set out to describe how service users as co-researchers can be turned into a reality and what are the opportunities and difficulties presented by this approach. These chapters followed the research cycle from beginning to end. Throughout the two chapters practical advice and examples were provided on how to undertake research with service users as co-researchers. Areas covered included research conception, the 'usual suspects', recruiting and training service user co-researchers, literature reviews, development of research tools, data collection, analysing the results, report writing and dissemination. From all of this it is clear that different service users will be able to collaborate in the research to different levels at different points of the research process. Whilst there is no a priori reason why service user co-researchers cannot be fully involved in all aspects of the research process some areas are easier to visualize than others. Thus, for example, it is easier to consider service user co-researchers being fully involved in the development of research instruments and data collection than it may be in the data analysis if this involves advanced qualitative or quantitative processes.

However, it should be remembered that most research teams include researchers with different skill sets to cover different aspects of the research project. If we do not expect employed researchers to be competent in all aspects of research we can hardly expect it of service user co-researchers. This relates back to the importance of not viewing service user co-researchers as being uni-dimensional when in reality they may wish to become involved to different degrees in different aspects of the process. If this is manageable within the research project it can be encouraged; if it is not manageable the potential service user co-researcher will have some choices to make.

These two chapters also emphasized the importance of training for service user co-researchers. The old adage that you only get out what you put in is certainly true. This cannot be underestimated; a 'formal' training programme at the start of the research project is important, not only for skilling up the co-researchers, but also for building a team ethos. Further training may be required once the research commences.

Involving young service users in research

This chapter was about sameness and difference. Many of the discussions about adult service users were also relevant for young service user co-researchers. There were, however, some pertinent differences surrounding the age and maturity of children and young people that do need consideration. In particular we highlighted the importance of the legal position of children and young people, the significant role played by 'gatekeepers', such as carers and schools, and the importance of child safeguarding processes for the research as a whole. However, many of the other practical, ethical and philosophical aspects of involving young service users in research concern issues of degree rather than kind. To this end it is important to consider children and young people as social actors in their own right, with the ability to change and to be changed by their world and to consider how they can actively become research partners in issues which impact upon their health and social needs.

Service user research futures

More than once during this journey we have commented that the involvement of co-researchers in research is both complex and contested. Beresford (2002) acknowledges that user involvement contains both liberatory and regressive potential. When we look to the future for service user involvement in research these conflicting directions are reflected in potential trajectories.

At one extreme there is potential for a continued token presence within the research community. This is where the service use co-researchers are 'included' as part of a research team to gain a research contract or to massage an external image of being inclusive. In reality the roles undertaken by the service user co-researchers are minimal and without impact. This might be the position where service users are recruited to administer a closed question questionnaire that has already been drawn up without them. Their only role is to administer pre-decided questions and take no part in the data analysis or writing up.

At the other extreme is a version of service user controlled research, conceived and implemented within a standpoint epistemology. This politicized model has the potential to replace one form of tyranny with another. It is just as bad to suggest that the only form of knowledge about service users can be that derived by and from service users as it is to claim that the only valid type of service user research is that undertaken by academically qualified researchers. Both have potentially justifiable knowledge claims to make which then need to be assessed in terms of how they answer their research question. To favour one at the expense of the other is to develop an unnecessary research schism and to miss out on the opportunities that knowledge from one will help to synergize the other. Or, as Nolan et al. (2007b: 190) eloquently put it:

> If we accept that differing types of knowledge and expertise contribute to a full understanding, then no one has privileged 'insider' knowledge, but everyone has differing knowledge from which everybody can learn. Herein lies the nub of the issue.

This leads to our third perspective, which as hinted above, is for service user involvement in research as co-researchers or in service user controlled research, to become an accepted and valued part of the health and social care research environment. For this to happen, service user involvement needs to remain honest, neither over-claiming nor under-claiming the strengths or weaknesses of the approach. In particular, we need more studies that can demonstrate the outcomes for this approach. Far too often a successful service user research project is assessed by the quality of the involvement, neglecting the impact of the outcome. Undertaking research is both a process and a task. If the process is right you have a positive feel about what you have done even if it has had no impact. To achieve the task at the expense of the process will result in a positive outcome, but disillusioned co-researchers and research respondents will be less likely to become involved in the future. The best result is when both the process and task are successfully achieved. This is the type of win-win scenario that those working towards involving service users in research need to be aiming for. This also requires research commissioners to be more informed about the realities of service user involvement in research so that issues of sufficient funding, resources and timescales are allocated to address the research question under investigation. If there is neither sufficient funds nor time service user researchers will, by necessity, have to cut corners and in so doing diminish the impact potential of the research and undermine claims for authenticity and credibility. Service user involvement as co-researchers or service user controlled research has the potential to both empower service users and also build on the knowledge that service users have of themselves and thus improve research outputs, outcomes and relevance for service users. In such a situation we are all winners – those who currently use services and the potential users of the future, and those not currently using services.

A note of caution, this type of research approach is not for everyone. It is absurd to think that any researcher will be able to work in such a manner as it is to assume that all researchers are just as capable with quantitative approaches as they are with qualitative ones. The government's current push, as outlined in its White Paper *Our Health Our Care Our Say* (Secretary of Sate for Health, 2006), aims to radically change the way services are provided, ensuring that they become more personalized to fit into service users' lives. It is also intended that service users become the major drivers for service improvement. It could be argued that involving service users in research is one way of helping to make this radical change a reality.

Final words

By now the reader should be aware that the author, although a supporter of involving services as co-researchers in health and social care research, is not naive about the changes that will be necessary. Involving service users as co-researchers is not a quick fix, nor a panacea, but a research approach that contains significant promise and hope that it can make a difference for the lives of those who use health and social care services. This book was written as an invitation to a debate. For those researchers and service users who are considering getting involved in such a project, it is hoped that this book will have provided you with some useful ideas and the impetus to try. There is no single 'prescription' for how to involve service users as co-researchers. We are all in the process of learning; we all need to be able to jettison that which has not worked in the past and experiment for the future. For those more steeped in such approaches it is hoped that the book will have resonated with some of your experiences, challenged others and acted as a stimulus for you to share your thoughts and views in the public arena. This area of research is a contested domain wherein debate and controversy signify vitality. There are many questions yet to be answered. We all have to be able to learn from, by and with each other. Ultimately, involving services as co-researchers or user controlled research should empower all of us. For this to happen, we need to value each other, service user, practitioner and researcher, whilst promoting a public debate about how involving service users as co-researchers can lead to improved services for all current and potential health and social care recipients.

References

A User Focus Monitoring Group (2005) 'A hard fight: The involvement of mental health service users in research', in L. Lowes and I. Hulatt (eds), *Involving Service Users in Health and Social Care Research*. London: Routledge. pp. 41–7.

Alderson, P. (1955) *Listening to Children: Children, Ethics and Social Research*. Barkingside: Barnados.

Alderson, P. and Montgomery, J. (1996) *Health Care Choices: Making Decisions with Children*. London: Institute for Public Policy Research.

Arnstein, S. (1971) 'A ladder of citizen participation', *Journal of the Royal Planning Institute*, 35 (4): 216–24.

Balloch, S. and Taylor, M. (2001) 'Introduction', in S. Balloch and M. Taylor (eds), *Partnership Working: Policy and Practice*. Bristol: The Policy Press. pp. 1–14.

Barnes, C. (2004) 'Reflections on doing emancipatory disability research', in J. Swain, S. French, C. Barnes and C. Thomas (eds), *Disabling Barriers – Enabling Environments*. London: Sage. pp. 47–53.

Barnes, C. and Mercer, G. (1997) 'Breaking the mould: an introduction to disability research', in C. Barnes and G. Mercer (eds), *Doing Disability Research*. Leeds: The Disability Press. pp. 1–14

Barnes, C. and Mercer, G. (2006) *Independent Futures: Creating User-led Disability Services in a Disabling Society*. Bristol: Policy Press.

Bassett, T., Campbell, P. and Anderson, J. (2006) 'Service user/survivor involvement in mental health training and education: Overcoming the barriers', *Social Work Education*, 25 (4): 393–402.

Beauchamp, T.L. and Childress, J.F. (1989) *Principles of Biomedical Ethics* (3rd edn). Oxford: Oxford University Press.

Becker, S. and Bryman, A. (2004) *Understanding Research for Social Policy and Pratice: Themes, Methods and Approaches*. Bristol: Policy Press.

Beresford, P. (2000) 'Users' knowledges and social work theory: conflict or collaboration?, *British Journal of Social Work*, 30 (4): 489–503.

Beresford, P. (2002) 'User involvement in research and evaluation: liberation or regulation'? *Social Policy and Society*, 1 (2): 95–106.

Beresford, P. (2005) 'Theory and practice of user involvement in research: Making the connection with public policy and practice', in L. Lowes and I. Hulatt (eds), *Involving Service Users in Health and Social Care Research*. London: Routledge. pp. 6–17.

Beresford, P. and Croft, S. (1993) *Citizen Involvement*. London: Macmillan.

Beresford, P. and Croft, S. (1996) 'The politics of participation', in D. Taylor (ed), *Critical Social Policy: A Reader*. London: Sage. pp. 175–98.

Beresford, P., Branfield, F., Taylor, J., Brennan, M., Sorteri, A., Lelani, M. and Wise, G. (2006) 'Working together for better social work education', *Social Work Education*, 25 (4): 326–30.

Bhaskar, R. (1979) *The Possibility of Naturalism*. Brighton: Harvester.

Borland, M., Hill, M., Laybourn, A. and Stafford, A. (2001) *Improving Consultation with Children and Young People in Relevant Aspects of Policy-Making and Legislation in Scotland*. Edinburgh: Scottish Parliament.

Brandt, A.M. (1978) *Racism, Research and the Tuskagee Syphilis Study (Report No. 8)*. New York: Hastings Center.

Branfield, F., Beresford, P., with Andrews, E., Chambers, P., Straddon, P., Wise, G. and Willcome-Findlay, B. (2006) *Making User Involvement Work: Supporting Service User Networks and Knowledge*. York: Joseph Rowntree Fellowship.

Bryman, A. (1988) *Quantity and Quality in Social Research*. London: Sage.

Butler, I. (2002) 'A code of ethics for social work and social work research', *British Journal of Social Work*. 32 (2): 239–48.

Butler, I. and Drakeford, M. (2003) *Scandal, Social Policy and Social Welfare* (2nd edn). Basingstoke: Palgrave Macmillan.

Butler, I., Scanlan, L., Robinson, M., Douglas, G. and Murch, M. (2002) 'Children's involvement in their parents' divorce: Implications for practice', *Children and Society*, 16 (1): 89–102.

Butt, J. and O'Neill, A. (2004) *Let's Move On: Black and Minority Ethnic Older People's Views on Research Findings*. York: Joseph Rowntree Foundation.

Campbell, J. and Oliver, M. (1996) *Disability Politics: Understanding Our Past, Changing Our Future*. London: Routledge.

Carr, S. (2004) *Has Service User Participation Made a Difference to Social Care Services*. London: SCIE and Policy Press.

Chappel, A. (2000) 'Emergence of participatory methodology in learning difficulty research: understanding the context', *British Journal of Learning Disabilities*, 28 (1): 38–43.

Children and Young People's Unit (2001) *Learning to Listen: Core Principles for the Involvement of Children and Young People*. London: CYPU.

Christensen, P. and James, A. (2000) *Research with Children: Perspectives and Practices*. London: Falmer Press.

Christensen, P. and Prout, A. (2002) 'Working with ethical symmetry in social research with children', *Childhood*, 9 (4): 477–97.

Citizens as Trainers, Y.I.P.P.E.E., Rimmer A. and Harwood, K. (2004) 'Citizen participation in the education and training of social workers', *Social Work Education*, 22 (3): 309–23.

Clandinin, D.J. and Connolly, F.M. (2000) *Narrative Inquiry: Experience and Story in Qualitative Research*. San Francisco: Jossey-Bass.

Clark, A. (2006) 'The mosaic approach and research with young children', in V. Lewis, M. Kellet, C. Robinson, S. Fraser and S. Ding (eds), *The Reality of Research with Children and Young People*. London: Sage, in association with the Open University: 162–80.

Clark, M., Lester, H. and Glasby, J. (2005) 'From recruitment to dissemination. The experience of working together from service user and professional perspectives', in L. Lowes and I. Hulatt (eds), *Involving Service Users in Health and Social Care Research*. London: Routledge. pp. 76–84.

Cocks, A.J. (2006) 'The ethical maze: Finding an inclusive path towards children's agreement to research participation', *Childhood*, 13 (2): 247–66.

Coghlan, D. and Bannick, T. (2001) *Doing Action Research: In Your Own Organization*. London: Sage.

Cowden, S. and Singh, G. (2007) 'The "user": friend, foe or fetish? A critical exploration of user involvement in health and social care', *Critical Social Policy*, 27 (1): 5–23.

Coyne, I. (1998) 'Researching children: some methodological and ethical considerations', *Journal of Clinical Nursing*, 7 (5): 409–16.

Crawford, M.J., Rutter, D., Manley, C., Weaver, T., Bhui, K., Fulop, N. and Tyrer, P. (2002) 'Systematic review of involving patients in the planning and developing of health care', *British Medical Journal*, 325 (7375): 1263–5.

Cree, V., Kay, H. and Tisdall, K. (2002) 'Research with children: sharing the dilemmas', *Child and Family Social Work*, 7 (1): 47–56.

Creswell, J. (2007) *Research Design: Qualitative, Quantitative and Mixed Methods Approaches* (2nd edn). London: Sage.

Crotty, M. (2003) *The Foundations of Social Research*. London: Sage.

CSCI (2007) *Benefit Barriers to Involvement – Finding Solutions*. London: Stationery Office.

D'Cruz, H. and Jones, M. (2004) *Social Work Research: Ethical and Political Contexts*. London: Sage.

Delanty, G. (2005) *Social Science* (2nd edn). Maidenhead: Open University Press.

Department of Health (1996) *Community Care (Direct Payments Act: Policy and Practice Guidance)*. London: Stationery Office.

Department of Health (1998a) *Modernising Social Services: Promoting Independence, Improving Protection and Raising Standards (CM4169)*. London: Stationery Office.

Department of Health (1998b) *Quality Protects: Framework for Action*. London: The Stationery Office.

Department of Health (1999) *National Service Framework for Mental Health: Modern Standards and Modern Service Models*. London: Department of Health.

Department of Health (2000a) *The NHS Plan: A Plan for Investment, a Plan for Reform*. London: Department of Health.

Department of Health (2000b) *A Quality Strategy for Social Care*. London: Department of Health.

Department of Health (2001a) *Research Governance Framework for Health and Social Care*. London: Department of Health.

Department of Health (2001b) *National Service Framework for Older People*. London: Department of Health.

Department of Health (2001c) *Valuing People: A New Strategy for Learning Disability for the 21st Century*. London: Department of Health.

Department of Health (2002) *Requirements for Social Work Training*. London: Department of Health.

Department of Health (2005) *Independence, Well Being and Choice*. London: Department of Health.

Department of Health (2006) *Reward and Recognition: The principles and practice of service user payment and reimbursement in health and social care. A guide for service providers, service users and carers*. London: Stationery Office.

Department of Health (2007a) *Local Involvement Networks Explained*. London: CSIP for the Department of Health.

Department of Health (2007b) *Progress with the Implementation of the Research Governance Framework in Social Care*, London, Department of Health, www.dh.gov.uk/en/Policyandguidance/Resaerchanddevelopment/A-Z_400 accessed 7/12/2007.

Department of Health (2007c) *Putting People First: A Shared Commitment to the Transformation of Adult Social Care*. London, Department of Health.

Department of Health, Department of Children Schools and Families, Association of Directors of Adult Services, and Social Services Research Group (2008) *Draft Research Governance Framework: Resource Pack for Social Care* (2nd edn). London: Department of Health.

Department of Health and Department for Education and Skills (2004) *National Service Framework for Children, Young People and Maternity*. London: Department of Health and Department for Education and Skills.

Department of Health and Department of Education and Skills (2006) *Options for Excellence: Building the Social Care Workforce of the Future*. London: Stationery Office.

Department of Health Press Release (2006) *£300m 'cash for change' initiative to tackle bedblocking*, www.dh.gov.uk/en/PublicationsandStatistics/PressReleases?DH_4010921 accessed 7th July 2007.

Dewar, B.J. (2005) 'Beyond tokenistic involvement of older people in research – a framework for future development and understanding', *International Journal of Older People and Nursing*, 14 (3a): 48–53.

Downie, R.S. and Telfer, E. (1980) *Caring and Curing: A Philosophy of Medicine and Social Work*. London: Methuen.

Easterby-Smith, M., Thorpe, R. and Lowe, A. (2002) *Management Research: An Introduction*. London: Sage.

Evans, C. and Jones, R. (2004) 'Engagement and empowerment, research and relevance: Comments on user-controlled research', *Research, Policy and Planning*, 22 (2): 5–13.

Freeman, I., Morrison, J., Lockhart, F. and Swanson, M. (1996) 'Consulting service users: The views of young people', in M. Hill and J. Aldgate (eds), *Child Welfare Services: Developments in Law, Policy, Practice and Research*. London: Jessica Kingsley. pp. 227–349.

Furedi, F. (2002) 'Don't rock the research boat', *Times Higher Education Supplement* (11 January), p. 20.

Giddens, A. (2001) *Sociology*, Oxford: Polity Press.

Gillon, R. (1994) 'Medical ethics: four principles plus attention to scope', *British Medical Journal*, 309: 184–88.

Glasby, J. and Beresford, P. (2006) 'Who knows best? Evidence-based practice and the service user contribution', *Critical Social Policy*, 26 (1): 268–84.

Godfrey, M. (2004) 'More than "involvement". How commissioning user interviewers in the research process begins to change the balance of power', *Practice*, 16 (3): 223–31.

Godfrey, M. (2005) 'More than "involvement": How commissioning user interviewers in the research process begins to change the balance of power', *Practice*, 16 (3): 223–31.

GSSC (2005) *Post Qualifying Framework for Social Work Education and Training*. London: GSCC.

GSSC and SCIE (2004) *Living and Learning Together Conference*. London: GSSC SCIE.

Haigh, C. (2007) 'Getting ethics approval', in T. Long and M. Johnson (eds), *Research Ethics in the Real World: Issues and Solutions for Health and Social Care*. London: Churchill Livingstone Elseiver. pp. 123–38.

Haigh, C. (2007b) 'Getting ethics approval', in T. Long and M. Johnson (eds), *Research Ethics in the Real World: Issues and Solutions for Health and Social Care*. London: Churchill Livingstone Elseiver. pp. 123–38.

Haigh, C. and Jones, N. (2005) 'An overview of the ethics of cyberspace research and its implications for nurse educators', *Nurse Education Today*, 25 (1): 3–8.

Haigh, C., Howarth, M. and Williamson, T. (2007a) *Research Ethics: RCN Guidance for Nurses*. London: Royal College of Nursing.

Hamlyn, D.W. (1995) 'Epistemology, history of', in T. Honderich (ed.), *The Oxford Companion to Philosophy*. Oxford: Oxford University Press.

Hammersley, M. (1992) *What's Wrong with Ethnography*. London: Routledge.

Hammersley, M. (1995) *The Politics of Social Research*. London: Sage.

Hammersley, M. (1998) *Reading Ethnographic Research* (2nd edn). Harlow: Addison Wesley Longman.

Hanley, B., Bradburn, J., Barnes, M., Evans, C., Goodare, H., Kelson, M., Kent, A., Oliver, S., Thomas, S. and Wallcraft, J. (2004) *Involving the Public in NHS, Public Health and Social Care Research: Briefing Notes for Researchers*. Eastleigh: Involve.

Hanson, B. and Mitchell, D. (2001) 'Involving mental health service users in the classroom: A course for preparation', *Nurse Education in Practice*, 1 (1): 120–6.

Harding, S. (1986) *The Science Question in Feminism*. Milton Keynes: Open University Press.

Hasler, F. (2003) *Users at the Heart: User Participation in the Governance and Operation of Social Regulatory Bodies*. London: SCIE.

Health Professions Council (2003) *Standards of Proficiency*. London: Health Professions Council.

Hewson, C., Yule, P., Laurent, D. and Vogel, C. (2003) *Internet Research Methods: A Practical Guide for the Sociological and Behavioural Sciences*. London: Sage.

Hill, M. (2005) 'Ethical considerations in researching children's experiences', in S. Green and D. Hogan (eds), *Researching Children's Experiences: Approaches and Methods*. Sage: London. pp. 61–86.

Hodgson, P. and Canvin, K. (2005) in L. Lowes and I. Hulat (eds), *Involving Service Users in Health and Social Care Research*. London: Routledge. pp. 48–65.

Holman, B. (2001) 'Upside down studies', *Community Care*, 12–18 April: 14.

Homan, R. (1991) *The Ethics of Social Research*. Harlow: Longmans.

Hughes, J. (1990) *The Philosophy of Social Research*. London: Longman.

Hughes, J. and Sharrock, W. (1997) *The Philosophy of Social Research* (3rd edn). London: Longman.

Hugman, R. (1991) *Power in Caring Professions*. Basingstoke: Macmillan.

Humphreys, L. (1975) *Tearoom Trade: Impersonal Sex in Public Places*. Chicago: Aldine.

Humphries, B. (2003) 'What else counts as evidence in evidence-based social work?' *Social Work Education*, 22 (1): 81–91.

Husband, C. (1995) 'The morally active practitioner and the ethics of anti-racist social work', in R. Hugman and D. Smith (eds), *Ethical Issues in Social Work*. London: Routledge. pp. 84–103.

IAASW and IFSW (2004) 'Global Standards for Social Work Education', www.ifsw.org/en/p38000208.html accessed 3rd July 2007.

Illich, I. (1976) *Limits to Medicine*. London: Marion Boyars.

INVOLVE (2006a) *Peer Reviewing Research Proposals: Guidelines for Members of the Public P2*. Eastleigh: INVOLVE.

INVOLVE (2006b) *Being a Member of a Commissioning Board: Guidelines for Members of the Public*. Eastleigh: INVOLVE.

Johns, R. (2003) *Using the Law in Social Work*. Exeter: Learning Matters.

Johnson, M., Buchanan, I., Long, T., Peacock, L. and Williamson, T. (2004) *Research Ethics: RCN Guidance to Nurses*. London: Royal College of Nursing.

Jones, A. (2004) 'Involving young people as researchers', in S. Fraser, J. Lewis, S. Ding, M. Kellet and C. Robinson (eds), *Doing Research with Children and Young People*. London: Sage in association with the Open University. pp. 113–30.

Jones, R. (1995) 'Co-opting carers and service users', *ADSS News* (April): 18–19.

Kellett, M. (2005) *Children as Active Researchers: A New Paradigm for the 21st Century*. London: ESRC.

Kirby, P. (1999) *Involving Young Researchers: How to Enable Young People to Design and Conduct Research*. York: Joseph Rowntree Foundation.

Kirby, P. (2004) *A Guide to Actively Involving Young People in Research: For Researchers, Research Commissioners and Managers*. Eastleigh: Involve.

Kirkpatrick, I. (2006) 'Taking account of the new managerialism in English social services', *Social Work and Society*, 4 (1): 14–24.

Lamprill, J. (2002) 'Asking for children's assent to take part in clinical research', *Clinical Practice Journal*, 9 (8): 1–4.

Leamy, M. and Clough, R. (2006) *How Older People Became Researchers: Training, Guidance and Practice in Action*. York: Joseph Rowntree Foundation.

Lewins, A. (2001) 'Compute assisted qualitative data analysis', in N. Gilbert (ed.), *Researching Social Life*. London: Sage. pp. 302–23.

Lewis, J. (2002) 'Research and development in social care: Governance and good practice', *Research, Policy and Planning*, 20 (1): 3–10.

Lockey, R., Sitzia, J., Gillingham, T., Millyard, J., Miller, C., Ahmed, S., Beales, A., Bennett, C., Parfoot, S., Sigrist, G. and Sigrist, J. (2004) 'Training for service user involvement in health and social care research: a study of training provision and participants' experiences (The TRUE Project)'. Worthing: Worthing and Southlands Hospitals NHS Trust.

Macquarrie, J. (1973) *Existentialism*. Harmondsworth: Penguin.

Marsh, I. and Keating, M. (2006) *Sociology: Making Sense of Society*. Harlow: Pearson Education Limited.

Masson, J. (2004) 'The legal context', in S. Fraser, S. Ding, M. Kellet and C. Robinson (eds), *Doing Research with Children and Young People*. London: Sage in association with the Open University. pp. 43–58.

McCartan, C., Kilpatrick, R., McKeown, P., Gallagher, T. and Leitch, R. (2004) *Disaffected young people and their experience of alternative education: Involving peer researchers in the research process*. University of Crete, Discussion Paper, European Conference on Educational Research, September 2004.

McClimens, A., Grant, G. and Ramcharam, P. (2007) 'Looking in a fairground mirror: reflections on partnerships in learning disability research', in M. Nolan, E. Hanson, G. Grant and J. Keady (eds), *User Participation in Health and Social Care Research*. Maidenhead: Open University Press. pp. 104–19.

McDonald, C. (2006) *Challenging Social Work: The Context of Practice*. Basingstoke: Palgrave Macmillan.

McGarry, J. and Thom, N. (2004) 'How users and carers view their involvement in nurse education', *Nursing Times*, 100 (18): 36–9.

McIntyre, A. (1987) *After Virtue: A Study in Moral Theory* (2nd edn). London: Duckworth.

McLaughlin, H. (2005) 'Young service users as co-researchers', *Qualitative Social Work*, 4 (2): 21–8.

McLaughlin, H. (2006) 'Involving young service users as co-researchers: possibilities, benefits and costs', *British Journal of Social Work*, 36 (8): 1395–410.

McLaughlin, H. (2007a) *Understanding Social Work Research: Key Issues and Concepts*. London: Sage.

McLaughlin, H. (2007b) 'Ethical issues in the involvement of young service users in research', *Ethics and Social Welfare*, 1 (2): 176–93.

McLaughlin, H. (2008) 'What's in a name: "Client", "patient", "customer", "consumer", "expert by experience" "service user" – What's next?' *British Journal of Social Work*, dol:1093/bjsw/bcm155.

McLaughlin, H., Brown, D. and Young, A. (2004) 'Consultation, community and empowerment: Lessons form the Deaf Community', *Journal of Social Work*, 4 (2): 153–65.

Miller, E.J. and Gwynne, G.V. (1972) *A Life Apart*. London: Tavistock.

Morgan, M., Calnan, M. and Manning, N. (1983) *Sociological Approaches to Health and Medicine*. London: Routledge.

Moses, J.W. and Knutsen, T.L. (2007) *Ways of Knowing: Competing Methodologies in Social and Political Research*. Basingstoke: Palgrave Macmillan.

Moules, T. (2005) 'Research with children who use NHS services: sharing the experience', in L. Lowes and I. Hulatt (eds), *Involving Service Users in Health and Social Care Research*. London: Routledge. pp. 140–51.

Neuman, W.I. (2000) *Social Research Methods: Qualitative and Quantitative Approaches* (4th edn). Boston: Allyn & Bacon.

Newman, J. (2000) 'Beyond the new public management? Modernizing public services', in J. Clarke, S. Gerwitz and E. McLaughlin (eds), *New Managerialism New Welfare*. London: Open University in association with Sage. pp. 45–61.

Newman, T., Moseley, A., Tierney, S. and Ellis, A. (2005) *Evidence-based Social Work: A Guide for the Perplexed*. Lyme Regis: Russel House Publishing.

NHS Executive (1999) *Patient and Public Involvement with the New NHS*. Leeds: Department of Health.

Nolan, M., Hanson, E., Grant, G., Keady, J. and Magnusson, L. (2007a) 'Introduction: what counts as knowledge, whose knowledge counts? Towards authentic participatory enquiry', in M. Nolan, E. Hanson, G. Grant and J. Keady (eds), *User Participation in Health and Social Care Research*. Maidenhead: Open University Press. pp. 1–13.

Nolan, M., Hanson, E., Grant, G. and Keady, J. (2007b) 'Conclusions: realizing authentic participatory enquiry', in M. Nolan, E. Hanson, G. Grant and J. Keady (eds), *User Participation in Health and Social Care Research*. Maidenhead: Open University Press. pp. 183–202.

Nursing and Midwifery Council (2004) *Standards of Proficiency for Pre-registration Nursing Education*. London: NMC.

Oliver, M. (1996) *Understanding Disability*. London: Macmillan.

Oliver, P. (2003) *The Student's Guide to Research Ethics*. Maidenhead: Open University Press.

Patton, M.Q. (1990) *Qualitative Evaluation and Research Methods* (2nd edn). Newbury Park, CA: Sage.

Pawson, R., Boaz, A., Grayson, L., Long, A. and Barnes, C. (2003) *Types and Quality of Knowledge in Social Care, Knowledge Review*. Bristol: Policy Press and Social Care Institute for Excellence.

Payne, G. and Payne, J. (2004) *Key Concepts in Social Research*. London: Sage.

Pearson, G. (1983) *Hooliganism: A History of Respectable Fears*. London: Macmillan.

Plomer, A. (2005) *The Law and Ethics of Medical Research: International Bioethics and Human Rights*. London: Cavendish Publishing Ltd.

Popper, K. (1980) *The Logic of Scientific Discovery*. London: Hutchinson.

Procter, M. (2001) 'Analysing survey data', in N. Gilbert (ed.), *Researching Social Life*. London: Sage.

Punch, M. (1998) 'Politics and ethics in qualitative research', in N.K. Denzin and Y.S. Lincoln (eds), *The Landscape of Qualitative Research*. London: Sage. pp. 156–84.

Reason, P. (1998) 'Three approaches to participative inquiry', in N.K. Denzin and Y.S. Lincoln (eds), *Strategies of Qualitative Inquiry*. London: Sage. pp. 261–91.

Reynolds, S. (2000) 'The anatomy of evidence based practice: principles and methods', in L. Trinder and S. Reynolds (eds), *Evidence-Based Practice: A Critical Approach*. Oxford: Blackwell Science. pp. 17–34.

Ritchie, J. (2003) 'The applications of qualitative methods of social research', in J. Ritchie and J. Lewis (eds), *Qualitative Research Practice: A Guide for Social Science Students and Researchers*. London: Sage. pp. 24–46.

Roberts, H. (2004) 'Health and social care', in S. Fraser, J. Lewis, S. Ding, M. Kelett and C. Robinson (eds), *Doing Research with Children and Young People*. London: Sage in association with the Open University. pp. 239–54.

Robinson, C. and Kellet, M. (2004) 'Power', in S. Fraser, V. Lewis, S. Ding, M. Kellet and C. Robinson (eds), *Doing Research with Children and Young People*. London: Sage. pp. 81–96.

Roche, B., Saville, P., Aikens, D. and Scammell, A. (2005) 'Consumer led research? Parents as researchers: the child health surveillance project', in L. Lowes and I. Hulatt (eds), *Involving Service Users in Health and Social Care Research*. London: Routledge. pp. 85–96.

Rogers, W.R. (2001) 'Constructing childhood, constructing child concern', in P. Foley, J. Roche and S. Tucker (eds), *Children in Society: Theory Policy and Practice*. Basingstoke: Palgrave in association with the Open University. pp. 26–33.

Save the Children (2004) *So You Want to Involve Children in Research?*. Stockholm: Save the Children.

Schutz, A. (1978) 'Concept and theory formation in the social sciences', in J. Brynner and K.M. Stribley (eds), *Social Research: Principles and Procedures*, London: Longman. pp. 25–36.

SCMH (2002) *An Executive Briefing on 'Breaking the Circles of Fear': A review of the Relationship between Mental Health Services and African and Caribbean Communities*. London: Sainsbury Centre for Mental Health.

Secretary of State for Health (2006) *Our Health Our Care Our Say Cmd 6736*. London: Stationery Office.

Shaping Our Lives Network (2003) *What Do We Mean By 'Service User' and 'User Controlled' Organisation?* www.shapingourlives/service%20user%20definition.htm.

Simmons, R. (2001) 'Questionnaires', in N. Gilbert (ed.), *Researching Social Life*. London: Sage. pp. 86–104.

Simpson, E.L. and O'House, A. (2002) 'Involving users in the delivery and evaluation of mental health services: systematic review', *British Medical Journal*, 325 (7375): 1265–8.

Smith, L.T. (1999) *Decolonising Methodologies: Research and Indigenous People*. London: Zed Books.

Smith, R., Monaghan, M. and Broad, B. (2002) 'Involving young people as co-researchers: Facing up to methodological issues', *Qualitative Social Work*, 1 (2): 191–207.

Snape, D. and Spencer, L. (2003) 'The foundations of qualitative research', in J. Ritchie and J. Lewis (eds), *Qualitative Research Practice: A Guide for Students and Researchers*. London: Sage. pp. 1–23.

Stanley, L. and Wise, S. (1983) *Breaking Out: Feminism, Consciousness and Feminist Research*. London: Routledge & Kegan Paul.

Steel, R. (2006) *A Guide for Reimbursing and Paying Members of the Public who are Actively Involved in Research* (2nd edn). Eastleigh: Involve.

Stevens, T., Wilde, D., with Kirby, D., Stewart, D., Wragg, D., Ahmedzal, S., Cunningham, D. and Darbyshire, J. (2005) 'Consumer involvement in cancer research in the United Kingdom, the benefits and challenges', in L. Lowes and I. Hulatt (eds), *Involving Service Users in Health and Social Care Research*. London: Routledge. pp. 97–111.

Strauss, A.L. and Corbin, J. (1987) *Basics of Qualitative Research: Grounded Theory Procedure and Techniques* (2nd edn). Thousand Oaks, CA: Sage.

Swallow, V., Coad, J. and Macfayden, A. (2007) in M. Nolan, E. Hanson, G. Grant and J. Keady (eds), *User Participation in Health and Social Care Research*. Maidenhead: Open University Press. pp. 151–65.

Tarleton, B., Williams, V., Palmer, N. and Gramlich, S. (2004) 'An equalising relationship: People with learning disabilities getting involved in research', in E. Williamson and M. Smyth (eds), *Subjects: Ethics Power, Knowledge and Consent*. Bristol: Policy Press. pp. 73–88.

Taylor, A.S. (2000) 'The UN Convention on the rights of the child: Giving children a voice', in A. Lewis and G. Lindsay (eds), *Researching Children's Perspectives*. Buckingham: Open University. pp. 21–33.

Thompson, A.S. (2002) 'My research friend? My friend the researcher? Mis/informed consent and people with development disabilities', in W.C. Van Der Hoonard, (ed.), *Walking the Tightrope: Ethical Issues for Qualitative Researchers*. London: University of Toronto Press. pp. 95–106.

Thurston, C. and Church, J. (2001) 'Involving children and families in decision-making about health', in P. Foley, J. Roche, and S. Tucker (eds), *Children in Society: Contemporary Theory, Policy and Practice*. Basingstoke: Palgrave in association with the Open University. pp. 224–9.

Torvey, M. (2006) *Why People Get Involved In Health and Social Care Research: A Working Paper*. Eastleigh: Involve.

Tritter, J.Q. and McCallum, A. (2006) 'The snakes and ladders of user involvement: Moving beyond Arnstein', *Health Policy*. 76 (2): 156–68.

Turner, M. and Beresford, P. (2005a) *What User Controlled Research Means, and What it Can Do*. Eastleigh: Involve.

Turner, M. and Beresford, P. (2005b) *Contributing on Equal Terms: Service User Involvement and the Benefits System*. Bristol: SCIE/Policy Press.

Tyler, G. (2006) 'Addressing barriers to participation: service user involvement in social work training', *Social Work Education*. 25 (4): 385–92.

Tymuch, A. (1997) 'Informing for consent: concepts and methods', *Canadian Psychology*, 38 (1): 55–75.

United Nations (1989) *Convention on the Rights of the Child*. New York: United Nations.

UPIAS (1976) *Fundamental Principles of Disability*. London: Union of Physically Impaired Against Segregation.

Wadham, J. and Storey, A. (2004) *There4me Evaluation: The Final Report*. Southampton: University of Southampton.

Waldham, J. (2005) 'From rhetoric to reality: the involvement of children and young people with mental ill health in research', in L. Lowes and I. Hulatt (eds), *Involving Service users in Health and Social Care Research*. London: Routledge. pp. 152–62.

Warren, J. (2007) *Service User and Carer Participation in Social Work*. Exeter: Learning Matters.

Warren, L. and Cook, J. (2005) 'Working with older women in research: benefits and challenges of involvement', in L. Lowes and I. Hulatt (eds), *Involving Service User in Health and Social Care Research*. London: Routledge. pp. 171–89.

West, A. (1997) *Participation and Attitude: Young People, Research and Dissemination* (Unpublished paper). Leeds Save the Children.

Williams, V. and England, M. (2005) 'Supporting people with learning difficulties to do their own research', in L. Lowes and I. Hulatt (eds), *Involving Service Users in Health and Social Care Research*. London: Routledge. pp. 30–40.

Wilson, A. and Beresford, P. (2000) ' "Anti-Oppressive practice": Emancipation or appropriation?' *British Journal of Social Work*. 30 (5): 553–74.

Young, A., Hunt, R., McLaughlin, H. and Mello-Baron, S. (2004) *Edge of Change: A Development and Research Project About the Implementation of Best Practice Standards in Social Work with Deaf and Hard of Hearing Adults*. London: RNID.

Young, A., Hunt, R. and McLaughlin, H. (2007) 'Exploring models of D/deaf service user involvement in translating quality standards into local practice', *Social Work and Social Sciences Review*, 13 (2): 25–39.

Abbreviations

CASP Critical appraisal skills programme – programme aimed to teach critical appraisals of research publications.

CRB Criminal Records Bureau, who check whether anyone has a criminal record from the age of 10 and if so records the nature of the offence and the criminal justice outcome.

CSCI Commission for Social Care Inspection – the statutory body responsible for the inspection of social care settings.

ESRC Economics and Social Research Council – a major provider of research grants.

GSCC General Social Care Council – the regulatory body for social work and social care.

GCSE General Certificate in Secondary Education – an academic award generally completed at the end of secondary schooling.

GNVQ General National Vocational Qualification – a more vocationally oriented qualification than the GCSE, also generally completed at the end of secondary schooling.

JSWEC Joint Social Work Education Conference – annual conference for stakeholders in social work education.

LINks Local involvement networks established in 2008 to promote local involvement in how health and social care services are provided in a local area.

NMC Nursing and Midwifery Council, the regulatory body for nursing and midwifery.

NIMHE National Institute for Mental Health in England, exists to improve the quality of life of people of all ages who experience mental distress.

MRC Medical Research Council – a major provider of medical research grants.

RAE Research Assessment Exercise – research selectivity exercise used to allocate university research funds.

RCT Random Control Trials – the 'gold standard' of quantitative research.

RSI Repetitive strain injury – injury often associated with repetitive actions like writing on a computer.

RNID The Royal National Institute for Deaf People is a national charity, campaigning and developing services for deaf and hard of hearing people.

SCIE Social Care Institute for Excellence – commissions, synthesizes and makes available up-to-date knowledge about what works in social care.

SURF Service Users Reaching Forward – a service user controlled organization for people with mental health difficulties which engages in research in the Durham and Chester-le-Street primary Care Trust.

SUTRA Service Users Training and Research Association – A not for profit organization run by long-term users of health and social services offering training and research.

UPIAS Union of Physically Impaired People Against Segregation – a campaigning organization for people with disabilities.

Index

Supporting researchers
for more than forty years

Research methods have always been at the core of SAGE's publishing. Sara Miller McCune founded SAGE in 1965 and soon after, she published SAGE's first methods book, Public Policy Evaluation. A few years later, she launched the Quantitative Applications in the Social Sciences series – affectionately known as the "little green books".

Always at the forefront of developing and supporting new approaches in methods, SAGE published early groundbreaking texts and journals in the fields of qualitative methods and evaluation.

Today, more than forty years and two million little green books later, SAGE continues to push the boundaries with a growing list of more than 1,200 research methods books, journals, and reference works across the social, behavioral, and health sciences.

From qualitative, quantitative, mixed methods to evaluation, SAGE is the essential resource for academics and practitioners looking for the latest methods by leading scholars.

www.sagepublications.com